SYNCHRONIZING
SUCCESS

SYNCHRONIZING SUCCESS

A PRACTICAL GUIDE TO CREATING
A COMPREHENSIVE LITERACY SYSTEM

MAREN KOEPF

FOREWORD BY TIMOTHY RASINSKI

STENHOUSE PUBLISHERS
PORTLAND, MAINE

Stenhouse Publishers
www.stenhouse.com

Library of Congress Cataloging-in-Publication Data

Koepf, Maren, 1956–
Synchronizing success : a practical guide to creating a comprehensive literacy system / Maren Koepf.
    p. cm.
Includes bibliographical references.
ISBN 978-1-57110-743-5 (alk. paper)
1. Language arts (Elementary)--United States. 2. School improvement programs--United States. 3.
Teachers--Professional relationships--United States. I. Title.
LB1576.K57 2008
372.6--dc22

                    2007051352

Cover and interior design by Blue Design (www.bluedes.com)

Manufactured in the United States of America on acid-free, recycled paper
14 13 12 11 10 09 08   9 8 7 6 5 4 3 2 1

To my husband, Paul,
who believes my dreams into reality

———

CHANGE IS HARD. CHANGE IS ANXIETY-PROVOKING AND NECESSARILY SLOW. MY OWN EXPERIENCE SUGGESTS THAT WHEN WE TRY TO CHANGE EVERYTHING AT ONCE, LITTLE THAT MATTERS ACTUALLY CHANGES. BUT SOMEONE HAS TO INITIATE AND SUPPORT THE NEEDED CHANGE. IF NOT YOU, WHO WILL? IF NOT TODAY, WHEN?
~*Richard Allington,* **What Really Matters for Struggling Readers: Designing Research-Based Programs**

CONTENTS

PART I A PRACTICAL FRAMEWORK FOR CONTINUOUS IMPROVEMENT

PART II SYNCHRONIZING COMPONENTS FOR LITERACY SUCCESS

Foreword

How do schools accomplish systemic, meaningful, and lasting change in their literacy programs? That is a very difficult question that is hard to answer. Systemic change in anything is never easy. In literacy education, change can be a particularly daunting task, as the change process must deal with, among other factors, various constituencies, conflicting expectations and goals, a multitude of philosophical and instructional orientations, different educational cultures, many and varied personalities, and, of course, the infinite variability of the children who are the recipients or beneficiaries of the literacy system. Too often, I have seen change that is haphazard, inadequately planned, inefficient, poorly implemented, ineffective, superficial, easily manipulated and sabotaged, and quickly abandoned for the next round of "systemic change." The result is lots of change, but little improvement in instruction, curriculum, and student achievement.

Books on effective literacy programs usually focus on one aspect of literacy education — policy, leadership, teacher professional development, instructional programs, materials, assessments, differentiation, and perhaps, most often, effective instructional methods. Each and every one of these components is important and needs to be addressed in a comprehensive approach to systemic literacy change. In my own work, I have tended to focus on assessment and instruction.

Despite my own comfort level with literacy assessment and instruction, I have often found myself wondering about how my focus on methods and materials fits into the larger picture of effective literacy programs for all students and teachers within a school's or district's total program for literacy education. To be honest, I find this a challenging task. I have found few, very few, examples of systemic literacy program development in the scholarly literature.

Enter Maren Koepf. I was first introduced to Maren Koepf in a graduate-level course on literacy education I taught at Kent State University. I found her to be a most interesting, thoughtful, and dedicated literacy educator. Moreover, the more I learned about Maren, the more I discovered how innovative and courageous she was.

Maren took on the challenge of leading her school's literacy program through systemic reform and improvement. *Synchronizing Success* tells the story of how Maren Koepf guided her school through this process to the development of the comprehensive literacy system at Moreland Hills Elementary School. In an engaging style, Maren provides a detailed road map for anyone wishing to embark on such a journey in his or her own school or school system. The first part of the book describes the principles that guided the change and the groundwork that formed the foundation of the comprehensive literacy system. She begins her story with a discussion of the vision and voice that sparked the change movement in her school, the comprehensive plan that was developed from that vision to achieve the desired outcome, the mechanism for maintaining growth and change through ongoing and thoughtfully planned professional development, and how all members of the school community were able to take on leadership roles in implementing the change. It is important to note that the story that Maren shares in this book is a collective one. Although she may have been the spark that ignited the flame for reform, the reform could not have happened without the buy-in and active support of the members of the school community—from school principal to teachers to support staff to parents. This book truly is the story of a school that opted to move away from the status quo.

The second part of the book provides readers with a look at what Maren calls the "nitty-gritty" of the system—the actual building blocks that were placed on the foundational groundwork. Chapters on assessment, instruction, and professional development describe how the various elements of an effective literacy program were developed and put into place at Moreland Hills Elementary School.

The final chapter is the one that I found most provocative. Through the publication of *Synchronizing Success*, Maren Koepf celebrates the work that was done in her school to make it a shining example of school literacy reform. However, in Chapter 9, Maren makes it perfectly clear that the comprehensive literacy system at Moreland Hills is a work in progress. As long as children enter this school, from kindergarten on up, the school can never be in a state of what is; it must always be in a state of becoming. Children change, teachers change, instruction changes, scholarship into literacy evolves. So too must school literacy programs. In this final chapter, Maren explores the future of her school's literacy program—not what her school is, but what her school might be in the future.

Although Maren explores her own ideas and her own agenda in this chapter, the invitation to the reader is clear—what can you do to improve the literacy system in your own school? In this final chapter, Maren explores untraveled ground. But, guided by thoughtful practice, sound theory, and empirical research into literacy instruction and literacy leadership, she is willing to consider the future in bold ways. Although some of these ways may prove to be false starts, they will eventually lead to the next generation of systemic change in school literacy programs. She accepts the challenge, and you the reader, whether teacher, literacy coach, specialist, principal, or school district administrator, are invited to accept the challenge as well. Are you willing to challenge yourself to engage yourself and your colleagues in the high-level, thoughtful, and intensive planning necessary to start the change process? Are you ready and able to engage yourself and your colleagues in the tough, nitty-gritty, in-the-trenches grunt work necessary to implement the changes that you plan? Maren Koepf is one educator who accepted those challenges, and her school is a better literacy place because of her efforts. If you are willing to consider those challenges, Maren's story provides you with a framework for making that change happen.

Timothy Rasinski, Ph.D.
Professor of Curriculum and Instruction
Reading and Writing Center
Kent State University

Acknowledgments

Synchronizing systems of literacy support within a district, school, or classroom does not evolve in a vacuum. It requires the collaboration and contribution of many wise thinkers. The same is true when it comes to writing a book about the success of such systems. While writing *Synchronizing Success*, I stood on the strong shoulders of exceptional leaders, researchers, and educators who persistently informed and expanded my professional vistas. I am forever grateful for the enduring support of my friends, colleagues, and family.

This book would not be possible without the resilient and gifted nature of the Moreland Hills Elementary School staff. I have been privileged to work and grow among dedicated educators who are willing to explore novel approaches to age-old problems and who can rely on one another to challenge entrenched beliefs with respect and open-mindedness. So I express my profound gratitude to the Moreland Hills teachers for plainly stating the obstacles that need to be removed; for demonstrating flexibility, skill, and innovation; and for raising the bar on professional learning.

I am also grateful for the leaders of our Orange City School District who look beyond traditional practices and structures to extend our district's capacity to serve the children. I appreciate the frequent opportunities I am given to learn cutting-edge perspectives on school reform and education research that inspire fresh solutions, refine my understanding, and empower my impact on student learning. I owe special thanks to Kelly Stevens and to Nancy Wingenbach. Kelly provided leadership as a school principal in launching our first "baby steps" in literacy reform and for mobilizing resources, networking contacts, and keeping the work in grounded perspective. And as the director of Educational Programs, Nancy's decision to reassign my role from an intervention teacher to a leader for professional learning multiplied our capacity for site-based professional development.

There are certain leaders in the profession of literacy education who are my steadfast mentors. They represent the vision, knowledge, and voice on literacy instruction I want to imitate in my work as an educator. Their reverent manner in the company of children cannot be overstated; their uncompromised advocacy for what matters most in support of striving readers and writers resonates as a call to purpose for me as an educator and a writer: Richard Allington, Carl Anderson, Lucy Calkins, Marie Clay, Ralph Fletcher, Stephanie Harvey, Peter Johnston, Ellin Keene, Lester Laminack, Debbie Miller, Katie Wood Ray, Tim Rasinski, and Susan Zimmermann.

I offer huge thanks to my senior editor, Bill Varner, and my managing editor, Erin Trainer, for trusting me as a novice writer. Bill pulled me out of the abstracts and into reality a number of times, and both patiently guided me through the publishing process. I'd also like to extend my gratitude to the team at Stenhouse who worked behind the scenes to attend to every detail and align the book's component parts into a unified whole. I had no idea!

It takes a rare kind of friend to agree to read raw manuscripts—chapters arriving out of order—and to honestly respond in the margins with comments pointing out murky writing or what parts are more valuable than others. I am indebted to my volunteer reviewers for their encouragement and honesty: Mary Croft, Carolyn Culbertson (my sister), Libby Larrabee, and Susan Steines. I laughed as Mary read in my office and repeated, "This is so exciting, actually interacting with the author as I read!" Rare, indeed!

Affectionately, I give thanks for my whole family. Mom and Dad taught me the significance of listening for the wisdom of children. My daughters—Britta, Laurel, and Jenna—have endlessly encouraged my writing and my leadership as an educator. And what can I say about a husband whose gift is to synthesize ideas and give meaningful feedback and who transforms a room (in each of our last three homes) into an author's office (complete with bookshelves, built-in file drawers, and a handcrafted desk) because he knows my dreams.

Thanks beyond words, to all, for believing in me.

Introduction

Genevieve is indeed a lucky girl. Like most five-year-olds, she arrived at her kindergarten classroom starry-eyed and eager to learn. But by midyear, her teacher noticed that Genevieve was not making the progress expected in basic literacy skills. To give her additional time and practice, Genevieve's teacher selected and applied specific classroom supports from a collective kindergarten source and also recommended Genevieve participate in a supplemental literacy group for the remainder of the school year.

Because Genevieve's specific academic struggles were thoughtfully documented by her kindergarten teacher and passed on to the next grade in a literacy portfolio, Genevieve was closely monitored throughout her first-grade year to ensure reading success. She participated enthusiastically in reading and writing workshop within her first-grade classroom because the books and tasks were "just right" and the instruction demonstrated strategic ways to figure out the tricky parts. Meanwhile, Genevieve's parents participated in a district academy where teachers and parents actively learned about seven comprehension strategies and worked in tandem to design simple and meaningful ways to practice these strategies at home. As a result of the insights gained at the academy, Genevieve's parents brought home piles of the suggested books from the local library; their conversations around the stories they read aloud as a family, in which they shared connections, confusions, and mental images, became deeper. At midyear, Genevieve's reading assessment performance indicated continued challenges with reading and writing. She was recommended for daily one-on-one expert instruction in Reading Recovery to supplement the differentiated instruction provided in her first-grade classroom. Genevieve's strategic knowledge for reading and writing accelerated even further, enabling her to finish that school year at the expected first-grade reading benchmark. And that's not all.

The strong foundation for Genevieve's second-grade year was established in kindergarten and first grade. A continuing workshop community of readers and writers provided Genevieve with a steady flow of descriptive feedback from her teacher while matching her growing reading skill with appropriate books. Knowing that Genevieve had come a long way with extra support, her classroom teacher coordinated goals and targeted classroom practice with a reading intervention teacher to solidify those gains and avoid regression. Second grade was a year of great strides—a year of delving into books with fascination and giggles and discovering characters as newfound friends. During the summer months between second and third grade, the local library and bookstores joined with the school's summer reading incentive program. They donated prizes for a reader's raffle, organized bins of books for readers of all levels, and gave each student a "reader's license" to take to the public library, making it fun and easy for parents and kids to find great summer reading.

By the time she met her in third grade, Genevieve's teacher was not aware that Genevieve was once vulnerable for reading failure. Genevieve's common assessment showed above-benchmark performance in the fall of third grade. In addition, Genevieve passed the state's end-of-year third-grade reading achievement test in October at an advanced level! (The state of Ohio requires third graders to take the end-of-year reading test in the fall for early identification of students' instructional needs.) Most important, Genevieve's mom and dad could barely keep enough library books in stock for their avid reader. Not only was Genevieve an accomplished reader, but she was infatuated with books, words, and learning all over again!

Clearly, Genevieve's "luck" was not by chance. Her growing success was strengthened by the ceaseless support of her parents and teachers and hastened by a schoolwide culture of routine monitoring, professional responding, and integrated efforts.

At Moreland Hills Elementary School, something remarkable is taking place. Over the past ten years, teachers and administrators have worked together to produce a learning network to support our students, our staff, and our parents. We have gradually changed the way we respond to young readers and writers, and we have steadily lifted our collective wisdom and commitment regarding what's best for children. From individual classrooms to the decisions and policies sent forth from the central office, we have generated an affirmative impact on student learning. Like the apprehensive peasants in *Stone Soup*, folks have gradually emerged from their isolated "huts"—their offices and classrooms—to generate mutual resources, solutions, and innovations. Through joint endeavors, we created a comprehensive literacy system.

Valued professionalism is now the norm at Moreland Hills Elementary School, along with a coherent focus on instructional intent. Through a series of collaborative grassroots initiatives, we have aligned key components for supporting student success. We identified common literacy assessments for comparing "apples to apples" when we describe our readers and writers. That element led us to determine appropriate benchmark reading levels for every grade level and every grading period. We have unified grade-level priorities for curricular objectives, distilling focused instructional attention from otherwise scattered content coverage. Now, a common literacy language guides discussions between kindergartners and fifth graders, parents and administrators, classroom teachers and reading specialists. We also share a timely and targeted system of responding when reading performance falls below certain levels so that every child receives the kind of time and support needed to succeed. Together, we are expanding the district's instructional capacity to maximize student achievement.

But it wasn't always this way.

My first month at Moreland Hills Elementary School felt like a chapter out of *Alice's Adventures in Wonderland*. I was hired as a reading resource teacher, and one job responsibility was to assess the first- and second-grade students "at risk" for academic failure. I was handed a list of the children referred by their previous teachers based more on each teacher's speculation than common indicators. Then four heavy boxes of standardized test booklets were delivered to my office with instructions from the district office to schedule a sequence of testing sessions using these booklets as math and reading diagnostics.

I was new to the district, so I did what I was told. Over the next two weeks, I gathered thirty first graders and twenty-eight second graders from sixteen classrooms to administer a series of norm-referenced tests. Students' eyes widened like puppies heading to the pound whenever I entered the classroom. They were the ill-fated few, and I was the dreaded testmeister of Moreland Hills. I led them to the library, where I administered each subtest by the book: no talking, no repeats, no stray marks on the answer sheet. It was excruciating—for them and for me. These six- and seven-year-olds were instructed to read each passage, then fill in a bubble beside the best answer. Passage? Bubbles? Some children could not read yet, and most could not understand why a teacher was not permitted to rephrase the directions more clearly.

To make matters worse, more tests awaited those who scored poorly on this first cycle of assessments. It was a long-established tradition to use the Gates-MacGinitie standardized test as a criterion for the Title I identification process. The right hand apparently did not know what the left hand was doing. Many of the same children from the first round of standardized assessments were then pulled in small groups to "read" more passages and fill in more bubbles. (By now they were becoming adept at bubbling.) Simultaneously, because I was a Reading Recovery teacher, I was required to assess individually the "lowest 20 percent" of our first-grade readers (some very familiar faces!) with Marie Clay's observation survey (Clay 1993). Although the observation survey tasks were vastly more informative and much more student-friendly, with interactive conversation and incrementally leveled storybooks, these represented the third set of assessments of these kids in three weeks!

Then, just when I thought the mad tea party was over, it came time to select students to enroll in Reading Recovery, an individualized literacy intervention aimed at accelerating the success of first-grade at-risk readers. But three classroom teachers informed me that it was their turn to "have" Reading Recovery. Apparently, in the name of "fairness" to classroom teachers, the support of the Reading Recovery program rotated each school year to only three rooms among the eight first-grade classes, regardless of the greatest student need. It seemed absurd, but nobody was laughing!

I am certain the intentions of the system were noble. It *is* important to gather baseline data on students' academic performance to tailor instruction to student needs. And soliciting referrals from a student's previous teacher makes good sense for monitoring a "watch" list from one year to the next. Moreover, no one would argue against the wisdom of providing intensive expert intervention in the primary years of schooling. But the separate decisions of district, classroom, and intervention operated on nonintersecting plans. So many standardized tests for primary learners were counterproductive, not to mention contradictory to our best intentions. Was a standardized test format developmentally appropriate with its answer bubbles, its rule of no repeats, and its one-size-fits-all reading passages? Would these tests really identify valuable targets for accelerating student learning? Shouldn't the referral process be grounded in common indicators of risk so that each teacher's referral is based on the same criteria? Might there be a way of assembling data about students' needs that was less emotionally charged with stress and failure?

All too often, school systems perpetuate a host of unconnected initiatives and inadvertently set up a competition between teachers, principals, or district leaders for time, attention, and resources. Unless deliberate attempts are made to identify systemic contradictions, to enrich the professional knowledge base, and to establish universal expectations for teachers, administrators, and students across a system, those isolated efforts offer nominal hope over the scheme of a student's school career. A comprehensive literacy system aims to bring the segmented actions that will support readers into alignment and integration so that students are not the ones left to untie the gnarly knot.

In *Synchronizing Success*, I combine current theory about school reform with the strong-holds of evidence-based literacy instruction to share what Moreland Hills Elementary School has done to unify efforts into an effective and efficient network of support for all learners. I place the organizational thinking of Michael Fullan, Richard DuFour, and Robert Marzano at a roundtable alongside the literacy legends of Lucy Calkins, Ellin Keene, and Richard Allington.

A *comprehensive literacy system* forms a dependable framework for continuous improvement that can absorb and integrate changes in technology, research, methodologies, and the revolving door of political directives. At its core lies a continuous cycle of attention to updating and refining common assessments, prioritized curriculum, quality instruction, and systems of responding to students at risk. That core is framed in principles of increasing *continuity*, providing *continuous professional development*, and inviting *collaborative leadership* to guide decisions and action steps and grounded in a literacy vision. For this reason, the book is divided into two sections: Part I establishes a vigorous frame and Part II corresponds to the cyclical core.

Synchronizing Success

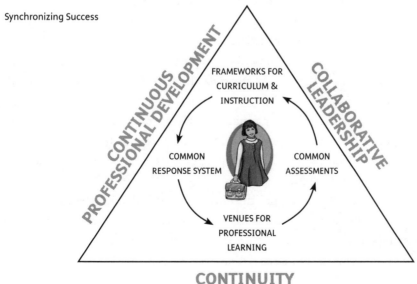

Part I, Chapters 1 through 4, explains the practical ideology that drives the decisions for each step we take. I emphasize the significance of maintaining a constant balance between communicating a defined literacy vision and seeking the voice of constituents to propel an ideal into action. Then I describe the three guiding principles—continuity, continuous professional development, and collaborative leadership—as the practical means used at Moreland Hills Elementary School to actualize a unified climate of support.

Chapter 1, "Uniting Voice and Vision," sets up the overarching conviction that the elements of vision and voice need to march in stride when facilitating change toward an integrated system. You can't move far from the spot you're in by standing and wishing your school could be better. In this chapter, I portray the overall vision of a comprehensive literacy system at Moreland Hills. I describe how defining an ideal vision can be significantly enhanced by regularly seeking opinions from all parties invested in helping students succeed.

One way to combat the haphazard nature of many fragmented acts is to take on one component of the system at a time, working collaboratively to increase continuity of practice. Chapter 2, "Continuity by Design," shows how continuity of professional resources, benchmarks, and instructional frameworks can help focus everyone's attention on maximizing learning: lessons are designed with qualities of good instruction in common, specific indicators of vulnerable readers are monitored, and a common literacy language describes student progress.

Chapter 3, "Continuous Professional Development," points to a significant influence on student achievement—the experience of quality instruction. Creating a plan to embed professional development into the school setting becomes a pivotal force for extending a district's capacity for high-quality literacy instruction.

Chapter 4, "Collaborative Leadership," describes a model that celebrates in-house expertise and empowers teachers to design and to generate the resources they need to manage exceptional instruction.

Our teachers have worked alongside our administrators to create rubrics, placing guides, and assessment systems. When new teachers observe veteran teachers, the vision and intention are reinforced twofold. Collaborative leadership taps into the collective intelligence and creates a synergy of shared ownership.

Part II of *Synchronizing Success* delves into the nitty-gritty of our comprehensive system. Chapters 5 through 9 detail the actual processes and illustrate specific resources to sustain common quality standards for assessment, instruction, and intervention and describe how we substantiate high professional standards with a wide array of site-based opportunities for professional learning.

Chapter 5, "Reclaiming the 'Professional' in Our Teaching Profession," depicts ways to capitalize on the wise experts in our midst. If we want our students to be lifelong learners, we need to offer our teachers multiple venues for professional reflection, rigorous study, and cutting-edge research. I scroll through a menu of nine models of professional development offered at Moreland throughout each year, each with distinctive pacing and purpose.

Chapter 6, "Apples to Apples: The Power of Common Assessments," focuses on the step-by-step process for developing our system for common assessments, flowing from preschool through grade five. It includes details about empowering representative teams of teachers from each grade level to critique and to recommend assessments that would be usable and informative in a classroom. Rather than purchasing a commercial assessment kit, teachers choose to do the research. They evaluate options and collectively determine measures of reading and writing that would effectively and manageably inform instructional decisions.

Additionally, I describe two resources sprouting from developing these assessments that communicate literacy gains from grade-to-grade: the Language Arts Assessment System database and a literacy portfolio folder that follow the child from grade to grade. The database displays, at a glance, student progress across six years of literacy learning. It helps us sort and generate data reports of information as needed to help guide our practice.

Chapter 7, "Standing on Strong Shoulders," shares the profound effect of consistent instructional expectations on scaffolding student success. Classrooms agree on the most essential elements to the curriculum and devote more time and practice to bringing these elements to mastery. Therefore, teachers from one grade can be assured that teachers from previous grades held the same focus of intent. This chapter will explain many of the resources created in collaborative teams to support consistent instructional expectations. Resources include guidelines for implementing guided reading, grade-level pacing charts, and the "essential learnings" for reading and writing instruction.

Chapter 8, "Response-Ability: Developing a Common System of Responding to Literacy Needs," is the most significant chapter and resource to school leaders. Three years ago, I facilitated a series of sessions, one for each grade level, to generate "If…Then" charts listing commonly problematic reading behaviors and generating a menu of classroom interventions to address each problem. That set of resources, along with a systemic plan for mutual response when students perform below established benchmarks, constitutes our literacy response plan. I explain the rationale and the steps for tailoring such a plan to your own setting. The appendix provides templates and resources that model the framework for implementing a common system for responding when students fail to make adequate progress in reading.

Finally, Chapter 9, "…and Miles to Go," projects possibilities for continued improvement into future hopes and dreams. Our comprehensive literacy system still has room for refining the existing program and extending the reach of continuity and professional integrity. Because we have systems in place, further improvements involve maintaining, updating, and expanding what already works well.

Sometimes you can work on a project so closely and constantly that you lose sight of your accomplishments. Writing Moreland Hills' story has restored my point of view. Recollecting the stories and conditions of our recent history has helped me realize how far we have come and how much good we have accomplished. Our assistant principal, Marilyn Mauck, was a first-grade teacher when the culture for literacy support at Moreland Hills began to shift. She recalls it this way:

> As a first-grade teacher, I was desperate to get some kind of training in best practices in the area of literacy. I can remember back when the only method for determining a child's reading level was your gut. However, many of us begged for a better system of accountability.
>
> When they say, "be careful what you ask for," this [workshop approach] seemed the perfect scenario. The transition time as we all moved into guided reading, word study, and interactive writing was a painful one for me. Not because I lacked confidence in guided reading, but relearning an entire new process would take time and practice.
>
> But with the supports in place, we were all able to make the transition. Without the professional development provided, we could not have done it.…The conversations were good and collaborative decisions continued to be made in regards to where students were in their reading: their strengths and weaknesses as readers, writers, and spellers. I don't recall one teacher defending the use of basals, though a few continued to "supplement" with basals until the books left the building.

As I look back, I could have been paralyzed by the magnitude of what needed to be changed. However, to paraphrase some relevant sayings, a leader has two choices: (1) to do what's always been done and expect different results or (2) to be the change you want to see happen. A system can move forward only when definitive steps are initiated.

Moreland Hills' journey toward a comprehensive literacy system is not without flaws. New and unexpected obstacles are revealed around every bend. Our adventure has drawn together teachers, parents, and administrators who once traveled on separate paths. I invite you to join the journey.

Part I
A Practical Framework for Continuous Improvement

1 – Uniting Voice and Vision

WE MUST NOW WORK ON THE QUESTION, "WHAT WOULD THE SYSTEM
LOOK LIKE IF IT DID KNOW WHAT IT IS DOING?"
—*Michael Fullan,* The Moral Imperative of School Leadership

L ake Erie is the size of Ireland. When my family first switched from years of sailing on a small lake in Pennsylvania to planning trips across Lake Erie, I was astonished to discover the vast areas where we could sail for hours with no land in sight. Without the compass on our Global Positioning System (GPS), it would be very disorienting. Therefore, to prepare for an excursion, we plot the coordinates for our destination and follow the recommended heading. In addition, we talk to other sailors and consult charts and location guides regarding provisions, safeguards, and attractions so that we can gain the most from our trip. The GPS readings keep us on track so we reach our destination efficiently, while the feedback from many sources—other sailors, charts, and wind indicators—makes the expedition more timely and enjoyable.

The same approach applies to navigating the immense waters of a comprehensive literacy system. Without a clear vision pointing to the intended goal on that distant horizon, you might find yourself heading in circles and visiting the same obstacles again and again. Without giving voice to so many valuable points of view, the quality and ease of the journey is compromised.

The combined elements of vision and voice create an amazing synergy. Their reciprocal interaction makes the change process more efficient and effective. The vision for a comprehensive literacy system names the intended destination and, like a magnet, draws all initiatives, resources, and decisions toward true north. That vision informs every decision— what essentials to value when critiquing instruction or materials, how to allocate funds meaningfully, what supports to establish to sustain high standards of quality. However, if a vision is to become more than a wish and a prayer, then the voice and involvement of invested role groups—teachers, parents, school leaders, students, community members, and organizations—are vital. The element of voice, in continuous improvement, ignites the action and energizes the momentum to reach the goal.

The vision becomes the driving force aligning all coordinates toward one destination, and the representative voices help determine a constructive itinerary.

The Vision for a Comprehensive Literacy System

Imagine a school in which every participant is valued as part of a highly effective system committed to maximizing student success at every level. What meaningful difference could educators make in the lives of children if we worked together to synchronize success? What might a school system look and feel like if the separate components supporting student learning were thoughtfully interconnected? How might our work be more effective if efforts to improve student learning were integrated across the district, within the building, and inside every classroom?

A vision starts with an ideal and can unfold with very real results. The ideal literacy vision at Moreland Hills Elementary School is to coordinate the work, resources, and commitment at all levels of the district to synchronize a collective pyramid supporting success for all learners:

Classroom teachers...

* Strive for high-quality classroom reading and writing instruction and know what it looks like.

* Rely on up-to-date professional research to inform daily decisions.

* Knowledgeably uphold the "why" behind instructional choices and are respected as experts in the field of education.

* Can depend on rock solid instruction of the previous grade as a foundation upon which to build subsequent learning.

* Have instructional resources readily accessible to make it enjoyable and manageable to design compelling lessons for a wide range of learners.

* Can expect increasing achievement scores to reflect students' deeper understandings and self-reliance.

At the grade or department level...

* Weekly time is held in reserve for colleagues to work together studying what influences student learning and troubleshooting ways to address student needs.

* There is a sense that the load and the commitment to do whatever it takes to help all children succeed are equally shared.

* Resources and solutions are exchanged to extend instructional effectiveness well beyond what anyone could accomplish through isolated efforts.

* A common pacing guide has been collaboratively developed as a time frame for cultivating and monitoring essential concepts.

* All members conduct a common set of informal assessments at established intervals through the year, keeping the instructional decisions tailored to the needs of the students.

* Collegial conversations reflect a proactive can-do approach to addressing obstacles to any student's success.

Intervention support teachers...

* Implement a new role. In addition to serving small groups of struggling learners, the interventionist offers a continuum of expert support to parents, teachers, and administrators.

* Coordinate lessons and goals with classroom teachers, resulting in more efficient and effective gains for students.

* Can accelerate learning for struggling learners due to a vital front line of classroom instruction and then amplified by a building-wide academic response plan. This systematic response plan guarantees that extra classroom or supplemental interventions are put into action when student performance falls below benchmark levels.

Building principals...

* Work to empower leadership and to extend the school's instructional capacity.

* Watch for evidence of quality instruction and offer descriptive and supportive feedback regarding expected norms.

* Facilitate opportunities for parents to join teachers in developing meaningful home-school connections, designing resources, and sharing suggestions.

* Routinely work alongside teachers to define and refine innovative solutions to identified issues.

* Expect universal benchmarks to help all teachers monitor student needs, differentiate instruction, and shrink achievement gaps. No child falls through the cracks because the indicators of students at risk are clear and because keen observers are everywhere.

At the district level,...

* Roles have been restructured to coordinate and substantiate literacy initiatives.

* Funds are reallocated to set key initiatives in motion.

* Expert professional development, for teachers and by teachers, is routinely accessible and customized to district goals and to what teachers need most to perform masterfully.

* A common literacy language interweaves clearer communication among the teachers, students, parents, principal, intervention team, curriculum director, and board of education.

* The school board's oath to teachers, parents, administrators, and students promises to do what it takes to remove barriers that impede quality instruction and to help increase the system's capacity to maximize student learning.

The system of support emerges as greater than the sum of its parts: Collaborative. Integrated. System-wide. A vision worth striving for! Although it seems idealistic, a vision of the preferred future is precisely the intent. That distant destination motivates commitment and draws disparate pieces of the big picture closer to a common purpose.

School reform expert Michael Fullan advises leaders of reform initiatives to "start small, think big" (Fullan 1997). The vision for integrating a district-wide support network committed to monitoring and advancing student learning is certainly thinking big. By positioning a comprehensive literacy system as true north, you set up the potential to engage all levels of a school district. That "big" vision serves as a catalyst for action and places a dependable point of reference in view as a target for all decisions affecting literacy achievement: curriculum, instructional implementation, student assessment, safety nets of intervention, and professional development.

There will undoubtedly be setbacks. Exemplary teachers will retire. State policies will add new layers of practice to be interpreted and assimilated into professional development. Changing demographics will mean changing supports. Budget cuts will squeeze dependable programming and necessitate innovative redesign. But vigilant attention to the ideal vision keeps your eyes focused on aligning systems, practices, and resources. The image of such an incredible ideal becomes a compass reading to steer the course back to the intended destination. Reachable? You bet. But it will not happen overnight.

Our first steps at Moreland Hills Elementary School were baby steps. We visited nearby districts to observe the implementation of instructional frameworks of interest. We offered monthly after-school inservices to anyone interested in attending. We studied and discussed articles examining instructional philosophy and practice. Some cynical teachers felt this was yet another attempt at faddish reform. However, their resistance communicated a powerful message: We needed to provide multiple entry points for people to join in the conversation, to dabble, and to study within a range of comfort zones, while reinforcing the expectation. At the culmination of a workshop or academy, I'd ask, "What piece of writing workshop are you willing to try this semester?" Teachers began to trust that even piecemeal attempts would be encouraged and supported and that the door was always open for them to attend study sessions.

We began with the folks who were able and eager to take part in study groups. From there, the contribution and commitment gradually spread through the halls, the classrooms, and into the district's central office. A group of kindergarten teachers would be chatting in the teachers' lounge about how their students saw themselves as writers and authors because of interactive writing. Colleagues would overhear the discussion and want to know more. Opportunities for learning and practicing components of a balanced literacy approach increased across classrooms and grade levels and so did enthusiasm. A groundswell of interest led to additional petitions for classroom demonstrations, common resources, or opportunities to problem solve dilemmas.

In the mid-1990s, I proposed a "Five-Year Plan" (Figure 1.1) for phasing in professional study and instructional expectations in deliberate increments. It served as a catalyst for creating a culture of continuous learning and growing that continues well beyond the initial five years. The plan framed a focus of our first actions one year at a time. It moved us off dead center and kept us from shooting in the dark at whatever looked good, interesting, or dazzling. We considered the assets that were within our reach, then incorporated intentional components of professional development, organizational structures, and collective resources.

Figure 1.1: Proposed Five-Year Plan for Unifying Literacy Practice

GOALS	**AMPLIFY LITERACY SUCCESS** Provide all students with engaging, congruent, relevant, and accelerative literacy instruction Develop a common "literacy language" for instruction, student observation and assessment, and professional discussion Affect cohesive standards, benchmarks, and philosophies of reading and writing instruction among and between grade levels Communicate to parents consistent standards, benchmarks, and instructional philosophies for literacy success
YEAR 1: INITIATE A SHARED VISION	**ORGANIZATIONAL STRUCTURES:** Form a preschool through fifth-grade literacy team to determine priorities for increasing continuity across the grades; begin by critiquing alternatives for consistent, simple assessments to be administered by preschool through grade two classroom teachers each fall and spring **PROFESSIONAL DEVELOPMENT:** Schedule article discussions on selected topics of literacy Provide after-school opportunities to learn about specific instructional techniques Schedule and facilitate site visits to districts implementing guided reading Offer a weeklong summer workshop on guided reading **RESOURCES:** Organize sets of leveled texts for first- and second-grade guided reading instruction Begin by leveling texts already in stock
YEAR 2: INVITE IMPLEMENTATION AND EXTEND TRAINING	**ORGANIZATIONAL STRUCTURES:** Continue literacy team, refining common assessments for kindergarten to grade two and extending the process to grades three to five Begin to shift roles of reading specialists to include shared planning for literacy instruction with classroom teachers (in addition to delivery of supplemental reading instruction) **PROFESSIONAL DEVELOPMENT:** Train teachers in skills needed for administering language arts assessment system (trial year) Offer a monthly book or article study for entire staff (in lieu of one staff meeting) Facilitate video-viewing and dialogue about qualities of literacy instruction Schedule periodic presentations on selected topics (determining powerful teaching points, nonfiction text structures, developing reading fluency) Join a consortium of professional development with neighboring districts Continue to offer running record practice sessions **RESOURCES:** Continue to expand the guided reading shared collection of texts, filling in text-level gaps and extending to levels for grades three to five

YEAR 3: **TRANSITION TO SHARED EXPECTATIONS**	**ORGANIZATIONAL STRUCTURES:** Administrative expectation for classroom implementation of specific components of literacy instruction, including routine use of running records, use of leveled sets of texts matched to a range of readers, evidence of explicit instruction of strategies for quality reading and writing Continue monthly literacy team meetings to monitor the implementation of assessments, recommend next goals for extending continuity, and project benchmark reading levels as standards for the end of each grading period Assign a literacy specialist to model instructional techniques and field questions about implementation **PROFESSIONAL DEVELOPMENT:** Continue site visits and/or add opportunities to observe in classrooms within our school Provide grade-level-specific release days or shared inquiries to study instructional techniques for balanced and comprehensive literacy instruction **RESOURCES:** Purchase leading professional texts to serve as mentor reference guides from experts in literacy instruction Identify benchmark exemplar titles within each level to be used for informal assessment throughout each school year
YEAR 4: **EXTEND TRAINING**	Continue the same structures, professional development, and resources from the previous year *And ADD...* **PROFESSIONAL DEVELOPMENT:** Provide bimonthly literacy forums for each grade level to facilitate ongoing collegial dialogue on problems and solutions regarding day-to-day implementation Send a group of teachers to attend the National Reading Recovery and Early Literacy Conference
YEAR 5: **FULL IMPLEMENTATION**	**ORGANIZATIONAL STRUCTURES:** Communicate administrative commitment to support training for new teachers Facilitate a mentoring focus on setting a climate for strategic thinking and an environment for reading and writing workshop Continue the Literacy Team work on increasing continuity **PROFESSIONAL DEVELOPMENT:** Continue article studies, book studies, along with occasional release days, presentations, or in-class modeling to practice intended techniques

You, too, can embark on a journey to generate a comprehensive literacy system. A general vision of increasing continuity of literacy policies and practice is enough to safeguard your first steps from perpetuating fragmented actions. You might not know expressly what you want it to look like or recognize all the details of what needs to improve. Don't let that stop you from stepping out of an old paradigm of resigned limitation and into one of co-constructive possibilities. The belief that you need the specifics before initiating action delays great reform efforts. Begin simply. Frame your five-year plan for initiating opportunities and inviting participation. Then refine your vision as you discover supportive organizational structures and as you gain insight from rich professional discussions about seminal research. A general sketch of how things might look someday is substantiated by an evidence-based knowledge of what matters most in maximizing learning.

From Random Acts of Good Intention

Every school seems to work relentlessly at arranging and rearranging the same set of components, trying to positively influence student learning:

* Professional development

* Assessment

* Curriculum

* Instruction

* Intervention

* Resources (material and personnel)

The arrangement changes with every change in leadership, but the issue of fragmentation remains. In most cases, these separate components play out as random acts of good intention. Intervention programs and classroom lessons designed in isolation give kids contradictory messages about expected reading behaviors. Sundry assessment practices measure information in terms that cannot even be compared, and professional development is linked only to an array of individual interests. It often feels as if the right hand doesn't know what the left hand is doing. Undoubtedly selected with good intention, each component ends up heading in different directions, as portrayed in Figure 1.2.

Figure 1.2 Disjointed Initiatives, or Random Acts of Good Intention

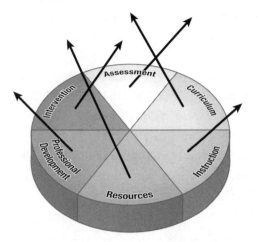

Constructing a comprehensive literacy vision means deliberately aligning the critical components of professional development, assessment, curriculum, instruction, intervention, and resources. The goal is to synchronize these components to maximize learning, as depicted in Figure 1.3. Part II of this book addresses these components in more depth: Chapter 5 addresses professional development, Chapter 6 addresses assessment, Chapter 7 addresses curriculum and instruction, and Chapter 8 addresses intervention. The component of resources is addressed throughout all the chapters of Part II as they relate to the other components specifically.

Figure 1.3 Comprehensive Literacy System

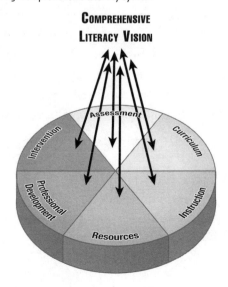

Voice Activated

In the case of school reform, the element of a shared voice transforms the ideal to the real. School systems clamor with voices. The state expresses mandates and standards of achievement. Parents demand excellence and personalized attention for a wide range of learners. Teachers ask for more time to plan and more support for differentiating instruction. Principals describe the latest changes in schedules, policies, and expectations. The central office leaders report the trends in demographics and the rationale for a new tax proposal. Students commiserate about difficult homework or boring classes.

An effective and efficient way to produce this seemingly massive shift across the system is by seeking and empowering a shared voice. Talking to the teachers, the parents, and principals helps to unveil the true assets and obstacles for the comprehensive literacy vision. To discover the conditions for a manageable classroom implementation, talk to the teachers. To design crucial home-school connections, let parents explain what they need from the school and how they might contribute as partners in education. Ask school and district administrators to join you in problem-solving. More important, gather these roles together to facilitate the kind of exchange that challenges ingrained beliefs and customary practices. These voices are the wellspring for making meaningful and unified decisions. By listening to diverse stakeholders in student achievement, communities are motivated to support the work that needs to be done.

Often we miss critical opportunities to connect to the mainframe. Everyone is invested in the big picture, and the more voices we include, the more pixels clarify that big picture. Yet, we make assumptions that dismiss the resources in our midst. Ignoring the voices of teachers or the potential contributions of willing parents can inadvertently instigate resistance. A well-intentioned initiative fades or fails because of a lack of input from those involved.

The element of voice in a reform effort honors differing perspectives and ensures a listening ear. Teachers want their expertise to be recognized as a valuable district resource. Administrators appreciate receiving a well-researched and methodical plan with nominal budgetary impact and a willing coordinator. Parents repeatedly inform us about what needs to occur to invite meaningful home-school connections, but we remain deaf to their words.

Your vision of a comprehensive literacy system can gain momentum in three powerful ways through the authority of shared voice:

1. Establishing a continuous loop of feedback

2. Motivating a community of innovators and problem-solvers

3. Instigating a tipping point

1. Establishing a continuous loop of feedback

To activate a comprehensive vision, you need to keep a finger on the pulse of what works and what does not. Here, the component of shared voice becomes a critical measure of the real obstacles along the path. A continuous feedback loop from key role groups helps literacy leaders make decisions that will take hold. Your constant role is to identify the barriers that impede progress and to find ways to remove those barriers for each role group (teachers, students, administrators, parents):

* Barriers to learning

* Barriers to implementation

* Barriers to participation

While listening to teachers express aggravations about the ineffective systems or insufficient supports for implementing commendable practice and recognizing the burdens and constraints placed on administrators to meet the state, district, and staff expectations, I realized certain barriers needed to be removed to liberate a new paradigm.

"I don't have time to go looking for the books or materials to go with every mini-lesson," argued Kerry after a lunchtime inservice to share resources for teaching the strategy in question. Kerry had to plan for four reading groups, three word study groups, and math and science, so her exasperation was evident. Kerry is an outstanding teacher; her plea was not about resisting change so much as requesting support. If we expect our teachers to maintain high standards of instruction, then we must provide them with extensive levels of support. In response to Kerry's expressed frustration, a list of library books suited for demonstrating specific comprehension strategies was generated. Instruction was not limited to these few texts, but the list alleviated Kerry's pressure with ready materials for manageable planning.

Teachers, parents, and administrators are dedicated to helping students achieve. Sometimes we simply have differing perspectives on *how* that should be accomplished. Each member of a school organization enters the challenge from a different vantage point, and those points of view need to be articulated. Throughout our process at Moreland Hills, various teachers or parents have either disagreed with decisions or made adamant requests for additional resources or clarifications. Rather than viewing these communications as adversarial, we recognize them as treasure troves, revealing obstacles that need to be addressed.

Allow the differing points of view to provide you with a more inclusive understanding of what needs to be better aligned, supported, or eliminated.

2. Motivating a community of innovators and problem-solvers

As the saying goes, if you always do what you've always done, you'll always get what you always got. The same is true if you always ask *who* you always ask. Soliciting voices across role groups can uncover astonishingly fresh solutions.

Our safety net team of reading interventionists stumbled across new ways to reduce the cycle of summer reading loss. We met monthly with a group of parents and teachers interested in collaboratively designing home-school partnerships. For decades, the public librarian would visit Moreland in May to speak to each library class about the public library's summer reading program. We ultimately discovered that many parents never heard of the program. The faculty had assumed that the students shared this information with their parents.

In response to this insight, the safety net team of reading interventionists met with local librarians and contacted community retail stores to initiate a summer reading incentive. Because of the innovative problem-solving among parents, teachers, local librarians, and merchants, students participating in summer reading receive prizes and awards, culminating in a grand celebration of reading when they return to school in the fall.

The role groups in your district represent your greatest resource for realizing the assets unique to your setting. These representative voices help everyone think outside the box. Time and again, the resources needed to support change are initiated and then created by collaborative groups who have expressed an interest and an expertise.

The input that comes from varying points of view can extend networks of contributors, expand resources for implementation, and generate an idea stream with fresh and surprising insights. It makes good sense to combine representatives from various role groups to generate innovative solutions and action plans for change.

3. Instigating a tipping point

In *The Tipping Point: How Little Things Can Make a Big Difference* (2000), Malcolm Gladwell refers to the tipping point as the moment when something unusual becomes common. At Moreland Hills, we have witnessed the tipping point phenomenon over and over again. Demonstrating comprehension strategies, using universal terminology and critereia to descrive reading behaviors, and embedding professional development within our everyday routines are now common practice across six grade levels. But this was not always the case. Each of these initiatives has traveled through a widening spiral of events leading to the tipping point of whole-school buy-in:

* Open invitation to study groups

* Dabbling in and reflecting on applied practice

* Teachers sharing the results of increased student engagement and achievement

* Collaborative development of resources for implementation

* Extended participation in further study

Our building-wide developmental word study approach began with a small group of teachers studying Kathy Ganske's book, *Word Journeys* (2000). A handful of teachers dabbled in applying this approach to a couple of groups of students. As teachers heard about the significant gains those kids made, they wanted to learn about this approach. Soon all forty teachers for grades one through five were asking for training. The original study group developed the resources to make implementation manageable and meaningful. Capitalizing on your trailblazers and mentors can influence a resounding call for change across the school.

For a change initiative to be successfully implemented, voices of all role groups need to be routinely and deliberately solicited. We need to invite dialogue among parents, classroom teachers, administrators, and interventionists to recognize the issues from diverse points of view.

Teachers frequently complain that certain students never turn in their homework. At a parent night presentation on study strategies, we ask participants to describe what we could do to help them help their kids. "Tell the teachers that two hours of homework is just too much," says a father exasperated with trying nightly to help his son succeed. A mother raises her hand to share, "I want my daughter to correct her mistakes on the tests sent home, but she won't do it unless the teacher says she has to." The conversation opens our eyes to the obstacles we inadvertently set up. Instead of pointing fingers in blame, we can agree on a shared plan of action.

Petitioning for opinions and feedback throughout the process helps create the comprehensive literacy system. Resistance to change diminishes, and opportunities for shared leadership increases. When you capitalize on the collective intelligence of stakeholders in your school community, a common voice arises from otherwise disparate perspectives.

Together, many voices can reveal barriers, unearth refreshing solutions, and cause a tipping point of high-energy and ever-expanding participation. What was once considered impossible becomes attainable and exciting! Deliberately extending your capacity for active listening and for responding in a timely fashion to the voices in your school must become your priority. The magnitude of establishing and uniting voice with vision from the start of a reform initiative cannot be minimized.

Balancing Voice and Vision

A literacy vision without voice leaves a leader high and dry and gives rise to angry resistors. The disconnected vision floats in midair with no grounding in the current realities of assets and obstructions and no plan of action. But having the strong element of voice without a defined vision won't cut it either. Such a condition sets off fragmented initiatives in contradictory directions, weakening the potential of otherwise gallant efforts.

Success unfolds gradually from deliberate attention to both vision and voice. The two serve as mutually supporting structures that guarantee the *flexibility* and the *endurance* of the created school culture. A system steady enough to hold up to years of changing personnel yet dynamic enough to shift when research reveals new truths about optimizing learning will grow stronger through persistent attention to both voice and vision.

Together voice and vision can unify the separate components affecting student achievement and can shape something truly vital and significant.

Building the Capacity for Continuous Improvement

Three guiding principles power the mechanism for ongoing improvement at Moreland Hills and help drive the vision forward throughout the process: (1) continuity by design, (2) continuous professional development, and (3) collaborative leadership. Each principle designates a focus area for strengthening and expanding the school's capacity for continuous improvement. At Moreland, we return to these three principles to guide decisions about next steps. Chapters 2, 3, and 4 will describe these guiding principles with practicality and detail.

2 —Continuity by Design

THE PROBLEM IS IF OUR TEACHING IS TO BE AN ART, WE NEED
AN ORGANIZING VISION THAT BRINGS TOGETHER ALL OF THESE
SEPARATE COMPONENTS INTO SOMETHING GRACEFUL AND VITAL AND
SIGNIFICANT. IT IS NOT THE NUMBER OF GOOD IDEAS THAT TURNS
OUR WORK INTO ART, BUT THE SELECTION, BALANCE, COHERENCE AND
DESIGN OF THOSE IDEAS.
—*Lucy Calkins,* The Art of Teaching Reading

I t's mid-May. Faculty mailboxes are crammed with piles of summer program fliers and memos about concert rehearsals and placement meetings. Assessment protocols and documentation forms sit in paper-clipped stacks on each teacher's desk. The list of parent phone calls to return seems to extend to the neighboring state. This is an important time to step back from the demands of closing out another year to take stock of the valuable work that has been accomplished. By doing so, we can set new goals while the work is still fresh.

The eighteen-member literacy team consists of grade-level representatives, special education teachers, reading specialists, and our assistant principal. We gather in the conference room for the last of our monthly sessions. Our team's mission is printed across the top of the end-of-year report: "The work of the MHS Literacy Team is to build continuity of professional knowledge, assessment, instruction, and resources for literacy among and across grade levels in ways that maximize student learning." First on our agenda, this May afternoon, is to review the literacy-related accomplishments for the year:

1. Established trimester benchmarks for reading, grades one through five

2. Developed a continuum of reading benchmark levels to illustrate the progression expected across grades kindergarten through five

3. Agreed on the terminology and definitions to use for genre instruction; developed grade-level genre wheels

4. Extended our community-guided reading book collection to include more nonfiction titles

5. Reviewed and revised the list of student data to be included in each student's literacy portfolio

6. Proposed summer writing projects for organizing updates to the assessment notebooks and for generating resources for planning mini-lessons

"Not bad for one year," exclaims Sallie, a kindergarten teacher with extraordinary commitment and bold ideas. And she's right. The list affirms the benefits of time well spent in respectful debate and collaborative action.

As a result of the work facilitated by this year's literacy team, grades one through five have more consistent tools and practices they can count on. We have standardized the expected reading levels to be reached by the end of each trimester. Performance below an established benchmark will signal teachers that a student needs more targeted instruction to accelerate progress. All teachers of kindergarten through grade five will collect samples of student work and assessment responses in student literacy portfolios according to a consensus of what teachers in subsequent grades want to see and use. Children transitioning from grade to grade or from classroom to intervention will use and hear a common terminology representing the genre categories and features. School leaders will allocate funds for supplemental materials based on shared decisions among teachers and administrators. Parents can more readily participate in progress conferences because a simple continuum will show them how an abstract term such as "Reading Level P" correlates to trimester expectations ranging from spring of kindergarten through spring of fifth grade.

But how did we get to such a place of collaborative effort and unified accomplishment? By inviting participation from interested role groups and by keeping three guiding principles at the forefront of our intentions:

1. Continuity

2. Continuous Professional Development

3. Collaborative Leadership

Three Guiding Principles for Continuous Improvement

Figure 2.1: Guiding Principles

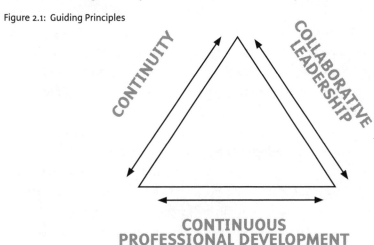

Continuity, continuous professional development, and collaborative leadership are the three guiding principles that drive the design for each year's action plan for continuous improvement (Figure 2.1). Designing increased continuity regarding the resources and practices we all use creates a common literacy language and common reference points for student achievement. Providing a wide array of continuous professional development raises the quality of our professional judgments and cultivates a culture of professional inquiry. Deliberately planning opportunities for collaborative leadership validates and harvests the resources of the many experts in our midst. The balance among these three principles propels our work forward, with high gains in literacy learning.

Over the next three chapters, we'll explore how each guiding principle helps actualize a comprehensive literacy framework tailored to your school. Let's look closely at the first principle: continuity.

Continuity: What It Is and What It Is Not

For too long, school systems have tolerated arbitrary assessments, hit-or-miss monitoring of learners at risk, and random acts of great teaching. Students are subjected to inconsistencies that can slow or stop their learning progress. We leave it to the kids to untangle the mess educators create such as contradictory expectations from different teachers. Are we just too busy to notice? We need to confront the brutal facts and examine the obstacles our own education system sets up for kids. As students transition from year to year or classroom to classroom, we expect them to interpret conflicting messages. One teacher exalts the importance of writing from your own experience; another one always requires students to write in response to assigned prompts. The social studies teacher records a zero every time homework is missing, yet the math teacher prods students until all assignments are turned in. The reading intervention teacher encourages students to examine a picture in the text for clues that scaffold word predictions, whereas the parent covers the picture and says that looking at the picture is cheating. It is often the disjointed system, not the content, that makes learning difficult for some children.

Schools have a moral responsibility to design and demand effective and efficient systems that advance student achievement. Increasing continuity of practice, policies, resources, and pedagogy from classroom to classroom, from grade to grade, and between role groups can significantly and positively affect student achievement within a school and across a district.

But increasing continuity *is not* about homogenizing professional discretion into robotic acts or scripted lessons. A classroom filled with diverse and eager learners hardly needs a one-size-fits-all program or a bland academic diet of canned mantra. Children's needs are seldom the same, so teachers' lessons had better not be either. With research pointing toward quality instruction as the most vital factor affecting student achievement (Darling-Hammond 2000), school leaders must invest in developing teacher expertise and professional judgment.

As opposed to implementing a series of top-down mandates, increasing continuity means we all work smarter by combining our efforts to maximize our effect on student learning. Common assessments, consistent expectations, customary routines, and a collective system for monitoring student progress can potentially transform our individual efforts into an exponential advantage. When educators work from a consistent knowledge base and common criteria for mastery, the students receive the gift of previous and parallel instruction.

Every year, I pose the question to the literacy team of classroom teachers, reading interventionists, and administrators: "What resources and practices can be made more consistent to advance the goals of our comprehensive literacy system?" More specific follow-up questions include, "What action plan might increase our school's capacity to provide high-quality instruction to all students?" and "What collective efforts among interventions, grade levels, parents, students, and administrators could fortify students' essential knowledge and deepen strategic thinking about reading?" Over the years, these questions have led to developing common resources, such as writing rubrics, pacing guides, reading-level benchmarks, and book collections, and it has guided our way to adopting instructional frameworks, designing professional development and training, and establishing timelines for responding to indicators of academic risk.

System Alignment for Powerful Practices

Districts orchestrate a zillion compartmentalized entities directly affecting students' literacy learning. Figure 2.2 lists just a few.

Figure 2.2 Some Policies, Practices, and Resources Directly Affecting Student Literacy Learning

* Practices for hiring
* Discipline policies
* Stated expectations (or not) to new hires
* Role of teacher mentors
* Training, support, and norms for new teachers
* Training, support, and norms for veteran teachers
* Expectations for instructional integrity
* Student assessments of and for learning
* Criteria for measuring student success or indicating academic risk
* Systems of response to indicators of academic risk
* Integration of supplemental interventions for struggling learners
* Professional inquiry and study
* Instructional approaches
* Communication of goals to teachers, administrators, parents, students
* Documentation practices
* District curriculum versus state indicators
* Supervisory and support roles
* Data collection processes and policies
* Discipline policies
* Methods of building relationships and connections with students
* Infrastructures promoting vertical or horizontal dialogue
* Technology integration
* Instructional integration across grade levels
* Transitions to new buildings
* Parent partnerships
* Homework policies
* Grading policies
* Allocation of funds
* Resources and materials for students and teachers

The problem lies wherever we continue working from scattered priorities and isolated plans. Central office administrators looking for programs that promise tidy statistics may not consider how well the scores inform instruction. Principals striving to maintain the status quo might overlook the vast variation of instructional content. Teachers presenting entertaining units on topics they enjoy may inadvertently rob students of the precious time and support necessary to master essential concepts. Parents wanting their children to like school and to make good grades might be unaware that the grade in one class reflects homework and effort whereas the grade in the next class reflects proficient knowledge. Students appearing disenfranchised and disruptive may feel that it's better to look lazy than stupid in the eyes of their peers. How can we begin to weave our efforts into an organized and deliberate set of actions? First, we must bring down the barriers that obscure student learning; we must destroy the walls that divide our innovations and segment our attention.

Only to Begin

In the summer of 2007, I attended a Model Schools Conference in Washington, D.C., where Raymond McNulty of the International Center for Leadership Education presented the keynote address on "Essential Learnings for School Reinvention." McNulty described the difference between *detailed complexity* and *dynamic complexity*. Detailed complexity is linear and inflexible. Each step is planned in great specificity (the way I plan a family trip to Disney World, down to a strategy for beating the lines). *Dynamic complexity*, however, approaches an action plan open to possibilities and acknowledges that unexpected stuff undoubtedly happens (which is my easygoing husband's approach to a vacation). McNulty suggested that leaders in education tend to wait until every detail is clearly outlined before launching a change initiative. As a result, few change initiatives ever successfully leave the drawing board. He explained that if the creators of Microsoft had waited for planned perfection, they would have missed an opportunity. Instead, they released version 1.0 with the understanding that new versions would offer updates as new technology became available. McNulty recommends that school leaders enter into a change initiative focused on *dynamic complexity*, ready to make a new version and move on. We educators must first get past the notion that an idea has to be perfect before we begin. *Detailed complexity* stifles action and probably explains why the educational system responds slowly to change compared with other organizations. So, consider the launch of the comprehensive literacy system as version 1.0.

The practices and policies listed in Figure 2.2 are brimming with prospects to strengthen and expand our collective impact on maximizing student progress. Consider the possibilities for accelerating student learning when the maze of systems, policies, and practices is reconfigured into coherent paths. Instead of approaching each as compartmentalized entities, boxed inside separate roles, suppose we look at policies, practices, and systems across a district with fresh, new vision, systematically pulling fundamental components into alignment?

Creating Consequential Results

Your entry point for creating a comprehensive literacy system will depend on the assets and interests identified within your school community. I have found certain actions of alignment to be more consequential than others because they create a surge of momentum and resources and establish foundational conditions for causing other elements to shift. For example, common assessments lead to data collection systems, data collection leads to establishing benchmarks, the established benchmarks lead to the study of instructional targets for various stages of reading, and instructional targets lead to common response plans. Bringing one component into alignment (such as developing common assessments) creates a craving for increased continuity in other related areas in a literacy system.

The hardest and most astonishing part for me has been trusting in the process of planning for dynamic complexity. This is hard because I am a bit of a control freak, and my comfort zone is in having the details planned and in order. But, whenever I follow a plan using dynamic complexity, I am astonished by how chance opportunities open doors I never knew existed. Although you thoroughly plot action steps for drawing another component of literacy education to align with the ideal vision, you remain open to unplanned bonuses or unforeseen detours. It is exactly that openness to possibilities and insights that builds the capacity for exponential, nonlinear acceleration of the process.

Four essential components have been the focus of our work in developing a comprehensive literacy system across ten years of continuous improvement: (1) common assessments, (2) consistent instructional frameworks, (3) curricular focus, and (4) intervention. Within each of these components lies potential for improvement ranging from far-reaching actions to simple but positive steps that can begin to bring scattered intentions into a common and focused alignment.

Chapters 5 through 9 will expressly delineate Moreland Hills Elementary School's processes for initiating extensive alignment within each component and will also share what was generated in terms of related resources and opportunities for professional development.

Through the lens of continuity and consistent expectations, we illustrate possibilities for working smarter within each of the four critical systems:

1. *Common assessments.* Tools, criteria, and time frames for assessing student progress are consistent among classrooms and reading interventions, across all grade levels, and within single grade levels. Rubrics, checklists, reading passages, benchmark levels, and indicators of academic risk are developed by faculty collaborations and are expected by administrators and school leaders as standard documentation.

2. *Consistent instructional frameworks.* Instructional implementation is grounded in a common set of guidelines defining quality practice, a common pedagogy, and consistent routines from grade to grade or classroom to classroom. Complementary approaches and goals unify the work between classrooms and intervention sessions as well as between reading instruction and science lessons. For example, at Moreland every classroom is expected to implement a reading workshop model and show evidence of differentiated instruction, extensive and engaging independent reading, and small-group guided reading instruction.

3. *Curricular focus.* District curriculum is tightly aligned with state standards. Although the specific terminology of standards differs from state to state, every state or province has an extensive list of learning objectives specific to each grade level and content area. Prioritized "power standards" (Reeves 2002) concentrate a concise and shared subset of these as a focus for instructional emphasis of time and attention. Pacing guides delineate a grade-level-recommended time line and sequence for introducing crucial concepts. Together, these are common points of reference as they increase each grade level's capacity to monitor and support student progress.

4. *Intervention.* Faculty and administrators embrace a culture of shared responsibility for the success of all learners, and they uphold a collective monitoring system with a specified time frame for responding to indicators of academic risk. All systems and supports for responding to differing student needs start from quality classroom instruction. A safety net team also advocates for struggling readers by planning and facilitating supplemental reading intervention, cultivating parent partnerships, designing professional development, and networking classroom materials and support.

Each of the four components contains opportunities, spanning large- and small-scale endeavors, for school leaders to initiate change toward a comprehensive literacy system.

Repositioning the Arrows

Incrementally aligning resources, professional development, and practice gives each change component time to take hold and gain ownership. Michael Fullan (1982) recommends taking a developmental approach, one or two steps at a time, that builds in more and more elements of the change over time. The job of a school leader is to work each year alongside district administrators, teachers, and parents to select which change component will hold the highest priority and to plan steps to redirect disjointed initiatives within that component to more closely align with the comprehensive literacy vision. This alignment is illustrated in Figure 2.3, where the dashed lines represent disjointed initiatives and the solid lines represent their alignment to the comprehensive literacy vision.

Each year at Moreland Hills Elementary, we pose the question, "What resources and practices can be made more consistent to advance the effects of our comprehensive literacy system?" Our responses inform what we will coordinate into a more unified direction. Fortunately, we've discovered that repositioning one major initiative (one arrow in Figure 2.3) inevitably draws another one or two related initiatives into alignment besides.

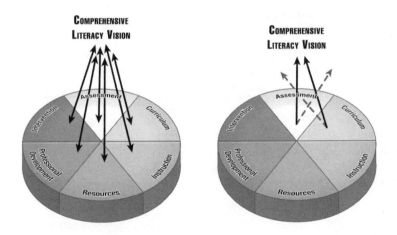

Figure 2.3   Shifting One Initiative (Arrow) at a Time to Align with the Comprehensive Literacy Vision

Continuity is one of three guiding principles that informs our action steps because it constitutes a system-wide commitment to maximizing student learning. It is the children who pay the price whenever the system neglects to align initiatives and structures in a common and intentional direction. Not one of us can close the achievement gap alone, regardless of how outstanding or hardworking we are. We must design ways to pool our expertise, our time, and our attention to work more efficiently and effectively. In every attempt to further continuity of resources, policies, and practices, we draw closer to the full vision of a strong and comprehensive literacy system (Figure 2.4).

Figure 2.4. Change Components

CHANGE COMPONENTS	POSSIBLE ACTIONS	ALIGNMENTS
COMMON ASSESSMENTS	Form a literacy team Develop a culture of shared responsibility for all students Develop common fall and spring assessments Determine useful classroom response assessments Provide training for taking running records Establish benchmark levels Create a database and/or portfolios for documenting progress Develop common writing rubrics Develop common grading policies Develop common homework policies	Across a grade level Between grade levels Classroom to intervention Teachers to parents Principal to teachers
CONSISTENT INSTRUCTIONAL FRAMEWORKS	Select a common pedagogy/framework (i.e., writing workshop, reading workshop, word study) Organize a common bookroom of leveled student texts Define expectations for evidence-based quality instruction Design self-evaluation rubrics for instructional implementation Develop instructional guidelines to abide by, including recommended blocks of time Align instructional evaluation/feedback with quality expectations Design or select complementary approaches Initiate a common "literacy language" of semantics or terminology Develop new teacher training and supports for expectations Identify and purchase a set of core professional texts as reference guides for each classroom teacher	Across a grade level Between grade levels Classroom to intervention Teachers to parents Principal to teachers
CURRICULAR FOCUS	Align district curriculum to state standards Identify prioritized standards as a dashboard of focused instructional emphasis and attention Develop grade-level pacing guides for each grading period in reading, writing, word study	Across a grade level Between grade levels Classroom to intervention Teachers to parents Principal to teachers
INTERVENTION	Design a pyramid of academic response Create a bank of classroom accommodations tied to reading behaviors Find/create opportunities for parent and community partnerships Instigate a literacy response action plan Determine a broad literacy plan for immediate response Form a safety net team advocating for struggling learners	Across a grade level Between grade levels Classroom to intervention Teachers to parents Principal to teachers

3 – Continuous Professional Development

PROFESSIONAL DEVELOPMENT SHOULD BE A PERSONAL PROFESSIONAL
RESPONSIBILITY AS WELL AS AN ORGANIZATIONAL RESPONSIBILITY. IN
OTHER WORDS, EACH TEACHER HAS A PROFESSIONAL RESPONSIBILITY
TO CONTINUE TO BECOME MORE EXPERT WITH EVERY YEAR OF
TEACHING. EACH DISTRICT HAS AN ORGANIZATIONAL RESPONSIBILITY
TO SUPPORT THE PROFESSIONAL DEVELOPMENT OF EACH MEMBER OF
THE FACULTY.
—*Richard Allington,* **What Really Matters for Struggling Readers:
Designing Research-Based Programs**

World renowned for extraordinary leadership in the medical profession, the Cleveland Clinic builds into its organizational culture many staff opportunities for continuing education and professional development. Weekly inservices demonstrate new techniques, procedures, or technology. Regularly scheduled release time for research updates and specialized training sustains professional growth for a highly skilled and knowledgeable staff. Patient outcomes are carefully charted, and collaborative teams determine a course of treatment. Systems of instructive support are designed so that professionals are constantly learning, monitoring, and evaluating high standards of practice while either mentoring or being mentored in distinct focus areas. Professional development is woven into the everyday fabric of the medical workday. Patients depend on and benefit from expertise and professional reasoning that draws on deep and extensive empirical knowledge. The medical profession recognizes that for an institution to survive and succeed, it is morally, legally, and economically obligated to invest in a continuous cycle of professional education.

Are we not morally obliged in the education profession to elevate expertise continuously so that students and parents can depend on teachers and administrators to be well informed and discerning about the lives of children? Since high-quality classroom instruction has enormous impact on children's academic achievement, schools would be wise to interweave professional study, reflection, and collective problem-solving into the culture and commitments of the organization. If educators are committed to inventing schools that make a difference, schools that beat the odds for student achievement and parent participation, we must embrace systemic professional development as a core investment.

While the principle of increasing *continuity* of practices and resources expands the community of mutual responsibility for closing the achievement gap, the second guiding principle of *continuous professional development* deepens the reservoir of knowledge, tools, and attitudes affecting student learning. Regularly examining research, posing questions, troubleshooting solutions, and practicing proven techniques increase the odds of significant literacy gains for students. Continuity alone may lead teachers to follow a scripted manual without understanding why the lesson is structured that way. But making continuous professional development a core part of school culture and design raises each teacher's ability to answer the "why" behind every action and to make the kind of informed moment-by-moment decisions that accelerate student learning. No software or commercial program can substitute for the differentiated instruction a master teacher can tailor to individual circumstances.

So each year in addition to addressing continuity by asking, "What resources and practices can be made more consistent to advance the goals of our comprehensive literacy system?" I also ask, "How can we support the comprehensive literacy goals with ongoing professional development?" More specifically: What professional development is needed for teachers, administrators, and/or parents to extend a common knowledge base and to expand what we know about making a positive impact on student learning?

Why Continuous and Embedded?

Embedding professional development into the daily school setting is a powerful force for enlarging a district's capacity to create and to maintain high-quality literacy instruction. Although bringing in an occasional outside consultant or sending groups of teachers to workshops may temporarily stimulate actions or fresh possibilities, the potential benefit to the school is no match compared with tailor-made continuous professional development. Site-based professional development can establish internal habits of reflection and initiation. Rather than climates of *blame and complain*, the pervasive response becomes *innovate and actuate*.

Dennis Sparks, emeritus executive director of the National Staff Development Council, cautions schools against overrelying on external sources for professional development. He warns, "Schools can benefit from knowledge and perspectives derived from the outside, but for many schools the balance between internal and external sources of knowledge and action has become so skewed that those in schools no longer see themselves as initiators of action or inventors of solutions to problems" (Sparks 2005, 12). By incorporating site-based professional development into the day-to-day routine, schools can shift faculty attitudes from resignation to renovation.

Offering teachers daily prospects to multiply resources or gain solutions invigorates professional energy. When teachers request ideas for instructing reading fluency, I schedule dates for before-school sessions in which teachers across grades pool resources on what they already do to support and instruct fluency. We look for strategies by such experts as Dr. Timothy Rasinski (2003) or Dr. Richard Allington (2006) to add to the list. The teacher-generated resource on fluency strategies is distributed to the faculty. These brainstorming sessions may inspire some teachers to frame classroom research on fluency. I meet with those teachers to review evidence of student performance, to help frame action research, and to identify relevant sources of support. Teachers eagerly take on new strategies and exchange ideas when they know they will receive an immediate and proactive response to requests for information, clarity, resources, or classroom support. Structures such as release days, reciprocal sharing sessions, instructional coaching, colleague observation, and resource development teams set up conditions for immediate and customized professional development.

In addition, if we expect high levels of professional performance from teachers, just as the Cleveland Clinic sets high standards of quality for their medical staff, we must fortify that expectation with a system-wide commitment to high levels of professional support. Every expectation needs to be backed with measures that guarantee success. When a new approach to reading instruction is introduced, it needs to be backed by the training and resources necessary for knowledgeable implementation. When habits of reflective practice are expected, opportunities for sharing reflections need to be included in staff meetings, evaluation meetings, and professional development days.

To realign our school and district toward a cohesive and comprehensive literacy vision, school leaders need to be selective and deliberate in sanctioning supports that reinforce that vision's intention as opposed to simply funding independent interests. Our comprehensive literacy vision includes complementary instructional frameworks, such as writing workshop, reading workshop, and developmental word study, because these frameworks emulate differentiated instruction, strategic comprehension, and critical analysis of author's craft. Therefore, we seek professional conferences and authorize professional development sessions that tie these approaches together and deepen the knowledge base for implementation. Otherwise, time, money, and resources might be spent on counterproductive measures.

The most efficient way to offer professional development is to establish a norm of continuous learning and to provide a variety of venues, such as mentoring, training sessions, use of protocols, or professional reading, for meaningful learning to occur at your school. The focus can be tailored to the instructional models and data specific to your setting. Then, you can enjoy the fringe benefits of designing a work environment that empowers and connects a community of learners.

The goal statement of the National Staff Development Council reads, "All teachers in all schools will experience high-quality professional learning as part of their daily work." *All teachers. Daily.* How is that possible when budgets are stretched thin and there is no literacy coach or staff developer?

Well, the first myth to debunk is that professional development depends on a person or a place. The idea that we have to wait until we can hire a professional developer and add on a room for professional development meetings may postpone action. When the perception shifts instead to realizing professional development as a habit or an attitude, countless opportunities reveal themselves.

Chapter 5 will detail a "menu of venues" for professional development, ranging from casual gatherings to formal planned academies, illustrating a variety of pacing and purpose. Figure 3.1 lists thirty nontraditional professional development workshops suggested by the National Staff Development Council (2005, 8). At least twenty suggestions have no overhead cost! So instead of sputtering "yeah, but," with excuses about insufficient resources, think "what if." Many possibilities require little more than the discipline of setting one's *attention* on professional *intentions.*

In our school district, we had to get past the traditional paradigm of perceiving professional development as an expensive line item on the budget by pushing clear of the notion that providing professional development necessitates either a registration fee or the cost of an outside expert. At Moreland Hills Elementary School, we began with article studies and reflection journals and rotated who would host discussions in their classrooms after school. Imagine, for example, asking the faculty this year to select one item from the list in Figure 3.1 to commit to as part of professional goals and practices: How can you support the comprehensive literacy vision with ongoing professional development? How will you increase the capacity for professional reflection and study?

Figure 3.1 The National Staff Development Council's Nontraditional Workshops

IF NOT A WORKSHOP, THEN WHAT?	
1. Conduct action research projects	16. Lead a schoolwide committee or project
2. Analyze teaching cases	17. Participate in lesson study
3. Be observed and receive feedback	18. Map your curriculum
4. Join a cadre of in-house trainers	19. Coach a colleague
5. Plan lessons with a teaching colleague	20. Be a mentor—be mentored
6. Consult an expert	21. Join a professional network
7. Examine student data	22. Use a tuning protocol to examine student work
8. Be coached by a peer or an expert	23. Maintain a professional portfolio
9. Lead a book study	24. Write an article about your work
10. Visit another school	25. Observe other teachers teaching
11. Write assessments with a colleague	26. Read journals, educational magazines, books
12. Participate in a videoconference or conference calls with experts	27. Participate in a critical friends group
	28. Do a self-assessment
13. Do a classroom walk-through	29. Shadow a student, a teacher, or another professional in the field
14. Give presentations at conferences	
15. Research on the Internet	30. Keep a reflective log or journal

You might begin by gathering a group to re-envision the multiple ways to integrate professional development and reflection practices before, during, or after the typical school hours. Consider an entry point or two where you might recapture time to revitalize and reshape a daily culture of professionalism:

1. Before students arrive

Co-planning

Consulting with a colleague

Integrating lessons across disciplines or roles

Collaboratively troubleshooting or networking ideas

Reviewing student portfolios

2. During school day

Performing action research

Framing a monthly or yearly building-wide professional focus/goal/topic

Coordinating in-house observations and reflections through a specific lens

Coordinating site visits with a partner district

Training sessions

Inviting guest speaker grade-level meetings (specialists in the building)

Encouraging co-teaching sessions

Posting enrichment ideas on shared server

Networking some troubleshooting online through blogs

Organizing parent forums on scheduled topics of interest

Referring to key professional texts

Providing release time for groups with a specific instructional or assessment focus

Reflecting on practice over lunch

3. After students' school day

Demonstrating one technique at staff meeting moments

Leading book/article study groups

Working on specific resource development in teams

Coordinating classroom walk-throughs to observe an environmental element such as word walls

Observing and critiquing student work samples

Mentoring new teachers

4. Summer break

Providing summer academies and/or training sessions

Encouraging/organizing summer project or resource development teams

Suggesting summer professional reading for staff

Encouraging book clubs with parent and student groups

Setting up Moodle dialogues with parents, colleagues, students

In *Powerful Designs for Professional Learning*, Lois Easton describes a number of methods similar to those listed above and writes, "This type of staff development is powerful because it arises from and returns to the world of teaching and learning. It begins with what will really help young people learn, engages those involved in helping them learn, and has an effect on the classrooms (and schools, districts, and even states) where those students and their teachers learn" (2004, 2).

What Do Teachers Need to Sustain Quality Professional Wisdom?

The ultimate goal in providing continuous professional development is to cultivate and sustain habits of discretionary wisdom among your staff. Daily educational decisions should positively improve levels of student engagement and success. Teachers hold enormous influence and power over young lives, whether or not their actions are intentional. The choice to raise awareness of issues or obstacles, increase appreciation for diversity, and instill knowledge of proven practices is no less than noble.

Wise discretion evolves from a place of empathy, experience, and knowledge. As professional development opportunities are designed, consider what the teachers will need to become keen observers, informed practitioners, and responsive advocates for all learners. What structures, resources, and purposes can be gradually introduced to expand a school's capacity for site-based professional development?

1. Structures that expand capacity for professional development

Skillful school and district leadership (consider many sources)

Variety of professional development options offered throughout the week, month, and year

Designated spaces for large-group professional development

Calendars posting professional development offerings

Instructional schedules that provide shared planning blocks with colleagues

Frequently stated administrative expectations for participation

Procedures for teachers to submit proposals of collaborative study or projects

Budget allocations for texts, materials, guest presenters, and/or food

2. Resources that facilitate professional reflection and critical conversation

Access to data reports directly applicable to setting classroom goals

Sources for professional articles on topics of interest

Space during the school day for teams to work

Access to computers

Rubrics for observing student work

Rubrics for teachers' self-assessment

Design qualities for lessons

Packets of instructional resources or resource templates

Contacts in similar and close-by districts

Reflection journals

Food/snacks

Purchase of professional texts for study and lesson resources

3. *Purposes for professional development in literacy*

Study the current evidence-based research of what makes a difference

Demonstrate application across flexible settings (i.e., content areas, intervention, grade levels)

Analyze data, target student goals, and design action plans

Self-evaluate and set professional goals

Challenge entrenched assumptions or stereotypes

Read novels used for guided reading; generate questions to spark discussion along with critical points in texts to linger and notice

Hone skills

Share multiple approaches

Generate solutions

Develop common assessments

Practice a skill (taking running records, conferring, blogging)

Learn a new form of technology to augment instruction

Observe technique, student response, teacher prompting, instructional language, instructional environment, management, logistics

Look at student work to determine a teaching point of focused feedback

Set instructional goals based on data/observation

Debrief with colleagues based on focused observations

Train teachers, parents, administrators

Strengthen community relationships and partnerships

Develop resources to help implement quality instruction or home supports

The possibilities are endless and can be specifically tailored to the instructional frameworks, issues, and interests unique to each school setting. So the second guiding principle to consider when planning action steps for continuous improvement and gradually constructing a comprehensive literacy system is *continuous professional development*:

What formats will merge professional development into everyday habits and routines?

When can we recapture time for professional development?

What will facilitate meaningful study for our teachers, parents, and/or administrators?

Providing an array of professional development, embedded into the everyday world of school and customized to specific priorities, sharpens professional judgment and cultivates a culture of lifelong learning. Continuous professional development deepens the integrity and fortifies the success of a comprehensive literacy system. As Roland Barth eloquently states in an interview with Dennis Sparks, "Real learning and accountability will not come from others inflicting their knowledge on teachers but from conditions created in schools that cause teachers to hunger after greater knowledge. That's when the learning curves go off the chart" (Sparks 2002).

4 — Collaborative Leadership

INVOLVING TEACHERS, ADMINISTRATORS, STUDENTS, PARENTS, AND
COMMUNITY MEMBERS IN SKILLFUL WAYS PROMOTES COLLECTIVE
COMMITMENT TO LEARNING FOR ALL STUDENTS. LAUNCHING SUCH A
SHARED VISION AND VISIONARY JOURNEY INTO SCHOOL IMPROVEMENT
UNITES US AS TRAVELERS ON THE JOURNEY TOWARD SCHOOL
IMPROVEMENT THAT IS CHALLENGING AND DEEPLY SATISFYING, AND
WHICH LEADS TO REMARKABLE RESULTS FOR ALL LEARNERS.
—*Linda Lambert,* **Leadership Capacity for Lasting School Improvement**

In July, Moreland Hills Elementary School morphs into summer space. Boxes of supplies barricade the mailroom. Carpet rolls and heaps of desks and bookshelves line the hallways. The drone of floor buffers can be heard in classrooms. Children in swimsuits and flip-flops, their shoulders draped in rainbow towels, march like ducklings behind a camp counselor.

Concealed within the leisurely façade of summer, small collaborative teams diligently develop building-wide resources to benefit students in upcoming years. A devoted contingent of fourth- and fifth-grade teachers meets on two consecutive days to generate guidelines for grading student performance in reading, writing, and word study. They want grades to represent consistent criteria across grade levels. A second-grade teacher meets in the guided reading book room with a special education teacher and a reading specialist to identify two texts per level as "landmark exemplars." These two texts will be benchmark student texts within our common inventory of more than 2,500 titles—texts that best exemplify each of the guided reading levels A–W (Fountas and Pinnell 1996, 2006) based on descriptors of text characteristics. The kindergarten through fifth-grade teachers will use these benchmark texts as informal checkpoints for taking running records and monitoring reading competence. A group of first-grade teachers get together to map out a pacing chart that names instructional touchstones in reading, writing, and word study for each trimester. They hope a shared resource for interventionists and classroom teachers will guide common priorities.

Many teachers volunteer each year to serve briefly as instructional leaders for particular projects. In small collaborations, they study, critique, and design literacy resources to benefit a range of grade levels. Some teams work on specific tasks in the summer; others share their time and talents to help mentor new teachers, to troubleshoot solutions, or to refine literacy resources during the school year. Important work is accomplished quickly, and during deliberations and background reading, the teachers gain a more profound understanding of the rationale behind the practice. The leadership role becomes a collaborative enterprise.

Collaborative leadership is the third guiding principle in reinforcing and determining action steps for a comprehensive literacy system. Whereas increasing *continuity* integrates practices, and coordinating *continuous professional development* creates a culture of professionalism, *collaborative leadership* solicits ownership and participation within the school faculty, the district administration, and the community. Collaborative leadership means that the major decisions—the solutions, the resource development, and the teaching—become leadership initiatives shared by many. Instead of depending on a solitary literacy leader, the comprehensive literacy system is fortified, through collaborative leadership, by an ever-extending leadership base. Teachers as leaders build a sustainable future. As teachers, parents, and administrators participate in co-designing integrated systems and resources, dedication swells. A self-perpetuating dynamic of professional innovation and shared problem-solving becomes the norm. Collaborative literacy leadership means many voices are represented in the decisions and many minds are invested in achieving the vision.

Perhaps the most powerful aspect of collaborative leadership is how it advances the comprehensive literacy vision. Creating project teams gets the work done faster and more efficiently. Combining diverse role groups, such as parents and teachers, administrators and interventionists, or special education teachers and classroom teachers, inspires fresh viewpoints, connections, and solutions. Encouraging collaborative groups to lead and innovate promotes deeper learning and meaningful teaching of the pedagogy. And the social interaction of working in a community rather than in isolation is much more gratifying.

Faster. Fresher. Deeper. More gratifying. For these reasons, the third question I consider when planning action steps is, "What opportunities for collaborative leadership will expand participation and advance the goals of our comprehensive literacy system?"

A Faster Rate of Accomplishment: Sharing the Load

To mobilize change and to gain momentum, many hands make light work. Leadership expert Noel Tichy advises, "The best way to achieve challenging goals is through teamwork. Where single individuals may despair of accomplishing a monumental task, teams nurture, support, and inspire each other" (Tichy 1997, 143). Early on in our literacy initiative, I discovered that as a literacy leader I don't have to accomplish this daunting change on my own. Dozens of people across role groups are willing and able to share the load.

Our district encourages collaboration by compensating teachers with a negotiated summer day-rate for time spent working on tasks that advance the district's vision and goals. This element of the teachers' contract turns out to be significant for extending the comprehensive literacy system. I maintain a teachers' wish list of resources year-round based on suggestions from book studies and professional development days, documenting what resources teachers will need to make expert implementation more unified and manageable. In the spring, our literacy team prioritizes these and proposes a list of projects to our director of Curriculum and Programming, who clarifies terms and sanctions support. As a result of teachers and administrators contributing time and sanctions, the whole faculty profits from collaboratively developed resources that enhance their practice. Consequently, broad-based ownership for our comprehensive literacy system thrives. To sustain the momentum of any initiative, teachers need strong administrative backing. By establishing a district infrastructure that annually reserves time and provides incentives to generate the necessary resources, we are collectively proactive year-round.

Mentoring, facilitating, planning, critiquing, modeling, networking, and developing resources for the literacy initiative do not have to depend on one leader. What a relief! Instead of sinking under the weight of all the responsibilities to actualize a comprehensive literacy system, I can trust and empower collaborative leadership to get the job done faster and more efficiently.

A Fresher Point of View: Shifting Old Paradigms

Through a series of fortunate events, the fates converged, which is what happens when diverse perspectives come together. Differing points of view challenge our assumptions and bring fresh possibilities forward.

A network of literacy coordinators from four neighboring districts met every six weeks for a half day to exchange and generate solutions on common issues. On one such occasion, Jodi and Kim described how Aurora schools make just-right reading levels of books easily available for families to check out during the summer months. Their innovative ideas for addressing the issue of access to appropriate texts planted a seed in my mind.

At a PTA advisory meeting, which included our principal and representative parents and teachers, a number of parents wondered whether our district would work with the local public librarians to teach our text-leveling system. At first, I was hesitant because I do not believe children should select books based on level. Then I saw the merit in sharing with our public librarians ways we encourage readers to choose appropriate texts. Parents also revealed that families don't always hear about the public library's summer reading program. Apparently, the news of a summer reading program is shared with the students during library time but does not always reach the homes. The suggestions changed my awareness, and ideas began to sprout.

Our assistant principal and a small group of teachers met with the public librarians to describe our leveling system. The group identified barriers to summer reading for many disadvantaged readers: insufficient library card registration, sparse inventory of suitable texts for emergent or early readers in the local library collection, few picture books and novels representing racial diversity, and inadequate supports for parents to help children find appropriate texts. We discussed preliminary action plans for how the library could support the school's efforts and the school could support the public library's efforts to encourage readers. In the meantime, a number of teachers were reading articles on the issue of summer reading loss and especially noted the significant impact of reading just five books over the summer break. Our weekly collaboration team of intervention teachers (professional learning community model) was already in the middle of planning a May parents night event. So the safety net team (the interventionists) capitalized on the recommendations from many sources, enlisting the support of the public library, parents, children, and local businesses, arranging the shards of inspiration into a mosaic of integrated response.

For the May parents night reading intervention, teachers specifically invited parents of challenged readers to bring their children for pizza, soft drinks, and cookies (with free child care provided by a local Girl Scout troop). The local public librarian prepared library cards for easy registration. We gave her a spot at the top of our agenda to describe and promote the summer reading program before we led families to the media center. There, parents learned and practiced ways to respond to a text while reading aloud with their children in pairs or triads. A wide range of donated books was sprawled across a table outside the school library, and every school-aged child was invited to choose one to keep.

In addition to parents' nights, a more monumental initiative was launched as a result of the previous series of collaborations: a building-wide summer reading incentive for kindergarten through grade five. We knew that summer reading loss was a recurring obstacle to closing the achievement gap, and parents explained that it was difficult to find books in the library that their children could easily read and that it was hard to motivate their children to read. So we rallied school and community contributions to draw more families to the local library without trepidation. We promoted the scheme during lunchtimes throughout the final week before summer break by challenging kids to commit to reading at least five books, because the research found that five books made a significant difference in eliminating summer reading loss. We showed the students gifts donated by local bookstores, ice cream shops, and fast food restaurants, and told them that everyone turning in a reading log in the fall indicating at least five books read could enter a drawing for these prizes. The safety net team created brightly colored "reader's license" cards (formatted like a driver's license, with the student's school photo in the corner) on which kids listed genres and topics of interest. The teachers coded each license with colored stickers to signal to the public librarian a range of text levels appropriate for the student's independent reading. The sticker color codes corresponded to colored-paper lists of trade books given to the local librarians so "just-right books" could easily be found for every reader. During the last week of school, an envelope containing the student's license, a reading log, a letter explaining the challenge and the raffle, and a reminder bookmark was mailed to every student's home address.

Just two weeks into summer, I received an email update from our local librarian. She announced that the numerous books she had ordered for emergent readers had arrived, and that she had prepared special bins of books matched to the reader's license color codes. She excitedly reported the influx of participation already under way.

As a result of a series of meaningful collaborations across role groups, fresher ideas blossom from tiny seedlings. Interaction among parents, community members, and teachers shifts old paradigms and challenges entrenched thinking.

Opportunities to make a significant difference do not fall into place accidentally. Deliberate invitations to step across established boundaries can unearth fresh possibilities. A closer look exposes the kinds of infrastructures that make room for real change to occur by crossing traditional lines:

Literacy coordinators routinely reach across districts to support one another and to pool ideas and solutions.

Advisory groups communicate concerns among administrators, parents, and teachers.

Community organizations are invited to contribute as partners.

School-based collaborative teams meet weekly to discuss research and to develop action plans to address identified issues.

Schedules are adjusted to enable collaborative groups to convene.

Local scout troops coordinate contributions with earning badges.

Administrators allocate funds for pizza as an investment in parent participation.

Classroom teachers know each student's reading level based on a common criteria and add a color-coded message to assist public librarians.

Librarians complement book collections to close an identified gap.

Parents and librarians help students find "just-right" books based on the student's interests and the teacher's recommendation.

Broad participation in collaborative leadership allows for creative problem-solving, for building new bridges of communication, and for tapping into unrealized networks of support. Fresh perspectives and innovations stir the dynamic and enrich the dialogue. An honest commitment to continuous improvement requires challenging the status quo.

Forming novel relationships highlight similarities and cultivate an appreciation of differences. Consequently, the lines dividing one group from another become more transparent. Old barriers between hierarchical positions dissolve as leaders across roles collaborate to plan system responses and to set priorities: parents and principals, district leaders and teachers, students and school leaders, local organizations and school districts. Competitions between districts transform into consortiums of shared resources when collaborative teams exchange site visits, establish a supportive network, or coordinate professional leadership. Gradually, the school culture transitions from compartmentalized role descriptions to a unified effort of maximizing student achievement.

A Deeper Professional Wisdom: Learning by Leading

Discontent with a commercial spelling program was emerging from the grade-level hallways. The lesson sequence seemed haphazard and depended on rote memorization, a stark contrast to the complex thinking strategies of guided reading. We decided to make the best of the adopted spelling series as we investigated alternatives.

Some teachers organized a visit to a nearby district where they observed a developmental approach to spelling; they immediately wanted to learn more. Classroom and intervention teachers formed a study group to examine *Word Journeys: Assessment-Guided Phonics, Spelling, and Vocabulary Instruction* by Kathy Ganske (2000). The study group held monthly forty-five-minute meetings before students arrived at school in which they negotiated reading goals and discussion topics. During the first year, this collaboration generated charts organizing developmental-stage knowledge and synthesized new information with practical application. A couple of teachers practiced the new approach with clusters of students and reported progress and hitches to the group each month.

Soon, we were hooked. The commercial options appeared blatantly flawed and limited in light of the theories we studied. In contrast to rote learning and assigned workbook pages, developmental word study was empirically grounded in differentiated instruction, active engagement, and higher-level explorations. In our classrooms, students with diverse spelling skills made chartable progress as their improved spelling was evident in their writing. The more we learned, the more apparent it became that we could not turn back.

In the process of applying the approach with small groups of students, it became plain that teachers would need the support of specific resources. It was unrealistic to expect teachers to generate four different word lists each week (we wouldn't want it to take away from time spent preparing for guided reading). Therefore, in the second year, seven teachers from the original study group committed time twice monthly to generate hundreds of word sorts matching a progression of features. The process of developing these resources deepened their understanding of the nuances within each feature. Recognizing the significance of this critical resource, district leaders arranged for these teachers to take extra time to further collaborations on the project.

Meanwhile, an invitation for classroom teachers to attend training academies on the features and the implementation of a developmental word study approach was distributed to forty classroom teachers in grades one through five. It was prearranged with our director of Curriculum and Programming that teachers who agreed to pilot this word study approach in the upcoming school year would be given a resource notebook of lists and a copy of *Word Journeys* (Ganske 2000) along with the team's ongoing support for general logistics.

All forty classrooms joined the training and committed to piloting the new approach. The amazing results in our classroom trials, and the offer of the resource notebook and training, motivated teachers to abandon the commercial spelling workbooks and to switch to the developmental word study approach.

During the pilot and subsequent years of implementing developmental word study (grades one through five), we offered brief morning forums each month for teachers to troubleshoot glitches, refine logistics, and give feedback about how the process worked in different circumstances. Soon, other districts recruited our teachers to present workshops on word study. An expression of frustration about existing conditions led to a colossal paradigm shift of instruction across five grades and uncovered significant site-based leadership.

Encouraging collaborative leadership is like adding Miracle-Gro to a garden. Existing talents will triple with brilliance and number. We all learn by leading. And the comprehensive literacy system benefits threefold: (1) relying on more site-based leaders extends your reach to offer more opportunities, (2) acknowledging leadership honors expertise and further endorses professionalism, and (3) having opportunities to lead deepens a person's grasp of the intended pedagogy.

In a school setting, opportunities to lead can range from quiet influences to outspoken presentations and from small commitments to full-blown projects. All forms of proactive leadership need to be nurtured (and sometimes redirected) and regularly acknowledged as viable contributions. Some opportunities for leadership in pairs or teams include the following:

Offering honest feedback

Actively listening to opposing views

Backing opinions with evidence

Sharing professional reflections

Sharing successes

Proposing possible solutions

Analyzing data to formulate hypotheses

Participating in action research

Mentoring a new teacher

Offering one's classroom for professional observations

Writing grant proposals

Collaboratively developing resources to share

Facilitating a book study

Organizing or preparing shared resources

Professionalism becomes widespread as teachers collaboratively delve into the whys and hows behind educational techniques. Site-based evidence from action research instills a contagious willingness among the faculty to risk change. And mentoring by our teachers for our teachers substantiates credibility and ownership of the instructional intent.

A collaborative leadership model, then, deepens the level of expertise in our midst and empowers the teachers in the trenches to design and generate the resources they need to make for manageable implementation.

A More Gratifying Workplace: Building Meaningful Relationships

A group of elementary parents and teachers gather after school for our February meeting. The conference table is strewn with beautiful picture books, samples of note cards posing open-ended questions to readers, sketches plainly illustrating each of seven comprehension strategies, and laminate samples from a local printer. We've been meeting monthly to refine a card game design and its distribution plan to engage all Moreland Hills families in practicing the same comprehension strategies taught from kindergarten through fifth-grade classrooms as a follow-up to a shared book study on *Seven Keys to Comprehension* (Zimmermann and Hutchins 2003). As we meet to test versions of the game activity, write a grant to fund the project, and refine the instructions and the printing logistics, we learn so much more than comprehension strategies.

During one meeting Angela, a devoted parent with three children attending district schools, expresses exasperation with some teachers' insensitivity. "Do they know how those huge homework projects put kids at a disadvantage? Not everyone has a computer at home or a color printer to crank out fancy brochures."

"That's true," agrees Shelby's mother, Melody, "and do the teachers realize how always asking kids to write about where they went during spring break discounts the value of just staying at home spending time with family?"

I am struck by the frankness of the conversation. Through months of working, laughing, and sharing together, these two circles, separating "us" (teachers) and "them" (parents), have opened to encompass a broader space where advocates for children mingle in honesty and action. These Moreland Hills parents trust me to express their frustrations and they candidly implore me to help get that message out.

Sometimes an unexpected discussion needs to supersede the carefully planned agenda. Angela's and Melody's statements point out important realities and awaken my personal reflections: How have I placed children at a disadvantage through mindless assumptions? How have I inadvertently contributed to the achievement gap? This new awareness enriches my life. Once nameless faces in the crowded hallways are now friends and colleagues sharing a journey.

Relationships matter. They make a difference in how we treat one another, and they satisfy the hunger for belonging and being heard. Bonds of trust and honest conversations present critical contributions for shaping and sustaining meaningful reform. Collaborative leadership shapes a school's culture into an intrinsically gratifying workplace of care, connection, and productivity.

Collaborative Leadership: The BOGO Deal

Collaborative leadership unites diverse perspectives, talents, and connections to cause a tipping point of real change. Time and again, I have witnessed how the outcomes of collaborative leadership outweigh the original objectives. I set out to teach parents about comprehension strategies, and I learn about ways teachers need to make assignments more considerate. We assemble across-grade-level teams to review content standards, and the dialogue reveals how each grade level can support mutual aims by grounding students in foundational concepts linking to a common knowledge base.

Our local grocery store sends out weekly advertisements plastered with buy-one-get-one-free deals, or BOGOs. I consider the guiding principle of collaborative leadership the BOGO deal. You encourage opportunities for collaborative leadership and you accelerate progress on meeting the goals for a comprehensive literacy system.

You can develop collaborative leadership by establishing dynamic infrastructures that

* petition feedback routinely,

* invite diverse participation and fresh solutions, and

* mobilize action.

Independent collaborative groups interconnect networks and solutions because everyone is heading in the same direction.

Driving the Vision Forward with Practicality

The three guiding principles and their questions drive the vision of a comprehensive literacy system on to the next action steps. The questions help us to name what is still incongruent, what knowledge or skills need to be bolstered, and whose voices are yet unheard.

1. *Continuity*: What resources and practices can be made more consistent to advance the goals of our comprehensive literacy system?

2. *Continuous professional development*: How can we support the comprehensive literacy goals with ongoing professional development?

3. *Collaborative leadership*: What opportunities for collaborative leadership will expand participation and advance the goals of our comprehensive literacy system?

To ground these three overarching principles in concrete and practical application, they need to be applied to components in schools that most significantly influence students' literacy success:

* Professional development venues

* Assessment

* Curriculum and instruction

* Intervention

Chapters 5 through 9 compose Part II of *Synchronizing Success*. I explicitly delineate how we, at Moreland Hills Elementary School, have used the guiding principles of *continuity*, *continuous professional development*, and *collaborative leadership* to develop the comprehensive literacy system within a pragmatic context. I describe how we have gradually and systemically developed ongoing adult learning venues, common student assessments, focused curriculum and instructional frameworks, and a pyramid of intervention responding to students "at risk." Each chapter also poses questions to guide you through a process of defining and designing a comprehensive literacy system that capitalizes on the talents and resources unique to your school setting.

Part II
Synchronizing Components for Literacy Success

5 – Reclaiming the "Professional" in Our Teaching Profession

REMEMBER THAT IN THE END IT WILL BE TEACHERS WHO MAKE A
DIFFERENCE IN CHILDREN'S LIVES. IT IS THE TEACHERS WHO WILL EITHER
LEAD THE CHANGE OR RESIST AND STYMIE IT. THE FOCUS OF SCHOOL
CHANGE HAS TO BE ON SUPPORTING TEACHERS IN THEIR EFFORTS
TO BECOME MORE EXPERT AND REORGANIZING ALL ASPECTS OF THE
EDUCATIONAL SYSTEM SO THAT THEY CAN TEACH AS EXPERTLY AS THEY
KNOW HOW.
—*Richard Allington*, **What Really Matters for Struggling Readers:
Designing Research-Based Programs**

Some of the richest experiences in professional growth can rise up out of the very center of our own everyday surroundings. Opportunities for thoughtful professional reflection and collaboration can be designed and facilitated by and for our teachers, acknowledging and capitalizing on the expertise in our midst. What makes site-based professional development so powerful is that the strands are woven right into the fabric of your school setting. The combination of empowering your teachers as leaders and embedding attentive professional support and study within the context of day-to-day routines creates a culture of vigilance and respect for quality instruction.

Walk with me through Moreland Hills Elementary School on a given day. You can witness the choreography of continuous and varied professional development:

A half hour before students arrive, a volunteer cluster of fourteen teachers sit on tiny kindergarten chairs, sharing responses to the month's article on closing the achievement gap. They casually exchange insights and connections raised by the reading and speculate about which small piece they might try in their own classrooms. They agree to report back next month on the results. A new article is distributed, and they adjourn to start a day of instruction.

Once the rush of incoming students settles into the hum of daily lessons, a literacy coach enters Carolyn's classroom. Carolyn is a new second-grade teacher, and a literacy coach demonstrates how Carolyn might draw her students' attention to a specific reading comprehension strategy. The coach thinks aloud while reading a picture book to Carolyn's students. Later in the day, Carolyn will meet with the literacy coach to discuss how the lesson and instructional language invited students to practice that strategy on their own. Carolyn will lead the next mini-lesson with the guidance and support of a literacy coach.

During a common planning time in the late morning, three science teachers meet with a reading specialist to plan ways to augment students' background knowledge on a topic before the unit begins. They consider salient concept vocabulary and devise interactive techniques for introducing a list of words students will encounter in an upcoming science unit on sound and light. Through brainstorming, they create specific text sets related to the science units. Their collaborative plan builds background knowledge so that all students begin the unit on a more level playing field. The teachers resolve to write a proposal for summer curriculum writing to extend this work into other science units of study.

After lunch, substitute teachers relieve two classroom teachers per grade level so that these teachers can work in the main conference room for the remainder of the day. The teachers pool resources and experience and analyze guided reading novels for instructional opportunities to heighten student awareness of text structures, literary nuances, or application of comprehension strategies. Our teachers are eager to make the transition from teaching the book to teaching the readers; time to become comfortable with a new way of planning for reading instruction supports that transition.

After school, a dozen teachers assemble in a fourth-grade classroom. Two intermediate teachers present samples of students' writing on transparencies. We use a protocol to guide observations about each student's writing, identifying a point of craft or convention that might constitute a learning opportunity.

This is all in a day's work.

Within every school setting, you'll find rare and remarkable teachers who demonstrate a cleverness and flexibility to respond to an array of student needs, who implement quality practice with the confidence of clear intent and experienced knowledge, and who raise critical questions about student progress and new curricula. These are the teachers who draw us all to a deeper level of professionalism.

According to Linda Darling-Hammond (2000), teacher expertise is the *most* critical factor for improving America's schools. Therefore, a district that invests in varied and continuing professional development will reap extraordinary rewards. Job-embedded professional development, tailored and targeted to the school's vision and unique circumstances, can magnify a school's capacity to strengthen student performance and can be accomplished by empowering the experts in our midst.

A powerful design for professional development intertwines a rich variety of offerings throughout the life and rhythm of the school year. My mother taught preschool children for more than twenty years. She loves to tell the story about the day she was in a grocery store when an astonished four-year-old student recognized her as he passed by. "Mrs. Rickert," he exclaimed. "You look just like a woman from behind!" It's true that some young children think that teachers live at school. Some teachers and administrators seem to spend more time at school than at home. But when we plan professional development opportunities, leaders need to respect that teachers do have lives and commitments beyond the walls of the school. Not everyone can or wants to spend Saturdays at daylong professional workshops. Instead, how can we embed productive professional development into the everyday workings of a school?

Three design considerations can help you plan a smorgasbord of dynamic professional support.

1. *Provide a range from simple and informal to structured and directed offerings.* Arrange for regularly scheduled gatherings around a simple topic or focus as well as for carefully planned sessions paced and supplied to the last detail. Some of the richest interchange and shifts in thinking spring out of collegial conversations by the photocopier.

2. *Provide for both horizontal and vertical interaction and conversation.* The fabric of student learning is strengthened by intentional continuity across and between grade levels, subject areas, and interventions. Assemble gatherings to augment, exchange perspectives, and refine decisions and resources that affect more than one group.

3. *Invite collaboration between differing role groups.* Parents, teachers, administrators, students, student teachers, special educators and interventionists, aides, and support staff shape the success of our students. Deliberate actions to invite collaborative learning and problem-solving can unveil refreshing surprises.

How do you design a model of professional development that is tailored and targeted to the needs of your own student population, that empowers and values the discretion of your teachers, and that makes effective use of the resources available?

Figure 5.1 describes nine models for professional development—a menu of venues—each with distinctive pacing and purpose, facilitated by teachers for teachers.

DESIGN ACADEMY	BOOK/ARTICLE STUDY	SHARED INQUIRY
One or more full days	75–90 minutes monthly	2–3 times per week for a month
20+ participants across role groups	Sign up for the year	Open invitation
Summer or during the school year	Dialogue on a common professional text focusing on application to classroom	Shared classroom research
Thorough exploration of a set topic and design for application in the classroom	Text(s) to be studied is provided	Explore implementation of best practice
		Collaborative design and instruction with a literacy coach
COMMON PROFESSIONAL RESOURCES	**CLASSROOM COACHING**	**TRAINING SESSIONS**
Universal set of professional texts and resource notebooks provided to each teacher, specific to each grade level	Short-term	1-hour to full-day sessions
	Guided practice with feedback	For new teachers or long-term substitutes
Some resources created by teachers for teachers	Specific instructional goals demonstrated by literacy coach	Specifically spotlighting instructional and assessment norms
	Teacher observes, then debriefs with coach	
PROFESSIONAL RELEASE DAY	**SITE VISIT**	**EXPERT FORUM**
Half-day or full-day sessions	1 hour to full day	30 minutes monthly
Grade-level teams propose release time to develop a shared resource or to learn more about a specified topic vital to raising student achievement	Small teams of teachers	Open invitation
	Visit on-site or to other schools or districts	Exchanging ideas around a pre-set topic
	Specific focus for observation	Troubleshooting
	Time reserved for debriefing	

Design Academies

The most structured of our professional development offerings is the design academy. Twenty or more participants across the district sign up for a seminar of carefully planned study and interaction on a theme that can stretch across many role groups. Middle school science teachers, English as a second language teachers, parents, and elementary reading teachers might all gather in one academy to focus on content-area reading or on grading practices. Often, this involves a book study where the text is provided a month in advance.

A guest speaker or a team of local leaders prepares a full-day curriculum. The morning session may focus on building a common knowledge base of issues or strategies. The pacing regularly invites adult learners to interact, practice, and exchange ideas. Then, in the afternoon, teams are instructed to design specific applications for the classroom or home.

For three years, we have held the *Seven Keys to Comprehension* Academy (Zimmermann and Hutchins 2003). With a group of first- to seventh-grade teachers and parents whose kids represent the gamut from striving readers to avid readers, we merge the partnership of home and school.

Throughout the morning, I model each of seven reading comprehension strategies. Following each demonstration, participants pair up and read stacks of picture books and text passages, from simple to sophisticated. As they read, they use sticky notes to mark where they make connections, sketch visualized images, and generate inferences. In this sacred space of shared experience, we sometimes cry or laugh as texts are brought to life. After lunch, teams of parents and teachers collaborate to design a clever and engaging game, brochure, or website parents and children can use together at home to extend the practice of comprehension strategies.

EXPERT Forums: Exchanging the EXpertise of Professional Education Resources for Teachers

EXPERT forums are monthly or bimonthly informal gatherings (usually first thing in the morning) lasting no more than thirty minutes. A focus or topic is preselected based on the school's goals and teachers' requests. Teachers drop in on dates when the schedule and topic works for them. The purpose of an EXPERT forum is to create deliberate time for teachers to share some obstacles of implementation and to troubleshoot solutions to common dilemmas collaboratively. Forums draw teachers out of their isolated classroom islands to discover the treasure of collective intelligence.

A forum facilitator schedules forums at routine times (e.g., the second and fourth Tuesday of each month, from 8:00 a.m. to 8:30 a.m.) and guides the discussion to flow from naming difficulties to exchanging solutions. I often keep a spiral notebook handy to jot down unresolved questions. Those questions help me frame the topic for the next forum, raise a question to our administrators, or design a subsequent staff development opportunity.

EXPERT forums provide a venue for a continuous loop of feedback from the teachers to the literacy coordinator regarding what is still needed for managing quality implementation. Change is hard. So when teachers are asked to change the way they provide instruction, it is important to make the new implementation as manageable as possible. One simple way to sustain the success of a new initiative is to create a safe place where voices of honest frustration and collaborative solutions are heard.

EXPERT forums are held in the cafeteria two mornings a month, one for kindergarten through second grade and one for grades three through five. On these mornings, square cafeteria tables are rolled together to form one common surface area with enough seating for about ten to fifteen teachers. Classroom teachers, our speech/language specialists, our English as a second language teacher, and interventionists may drop in during the half hour before students arrive to exchange ideas and questions about the specified topic. The group remains focused and engaged in casual but professional dialogue. We offer each other the benefit of practiced solutions and prominent questions about implementing excellent instruction.

The topics this month stemmed from a recent academy on Richard Allington's book, *What Really Matters for Struggling Readers* (2006). Much enthusiasm had resulted from our discussions about Allington's summarizing research regarding what really makes a difference in accelerating literacy development. In response, book study participants suggested we follow up by providing time for cross-grade-level groups to generate possibilities for increasing the volume of student reading time or to consider ways to deepen our conversations about literature.

Not everyone who joins us has participated in the book study, but because of their experience and interest, all have plenty to contribute. The sharing of ideas enhances our professional connection. To set the stage with a brief summary of one principle, I say: "Richard Allington has thoroughly studied and consolidated decades of educational research to determine principles of instruction that significantly increase reading progress. One principle we will focus on today is the idea that the more kids read, the better readers they become. What have you tried and what might we consider to increase the volume of reading opportunities for our students?"

Barb is a kindergarten teacher eager to share a system that works well for her students. "I hang a bag on the back of each student's chair and fill each one with books appropriate for their reading level. That way, whenever kids have five or ten minutes or when they first arrive, they know to go to their book bags for quiet reading."

Several teachers jump in with additional ideas while I record a list on a chart. It is all very informal, and there is a different combination of minds at each forum. You join in when it works for your schedule. The sounds of students in the hall signal the end of our informal conversation. I promise to type up our suggestions and questions and send an attachment as a resource.

Book/Article Studies

Our study groups meet monthly for a little over an hour, allowing time in between sessions to read and to respond to the selected text. Sometimes two or three book study groups are going at once. Perhaps there is a building-wide focus (such as comprehension strategies or writer's workshop), and the books selected are best suited to either primary or intermediate grades.

Teachers usually recommend textbooks at the end of the previous school year so that books can be purchased over the summer. For the article study group, members submit articles of interest from various professional sources, and copies are distributed the month before the discussion. Snacks are also served. We rotate study group meetings to different classrooms so that we can see how different teachers set the stage for learning.

An agenda or protocol helps to guide the discussion and to encourage participation. We begin with five minutes of quiet review of the text. If the reading assignment was divided into portions for different groups, I invite each group to summarize key ideas and to share their responses to the reading. Questions and comments are solicited before we move to another section. Issues we want to discuss are written on a chart, called the "parking lot," and we return to them after the text has been summarized. After each group presentation, we generate possible implications and applications or return to select issues on the chart.

The book/article discussions raise the level of professionalism among our staff. Text study groups are as important for gathering socially as for forming a learning community. Discussions sometimes focus on controversial points of view, yet we practice honoring varying perspectives and often stretch beyond our comfort zones. This shared opportunity deepens our understanding, develops a common language, and fortifies mutual respect.

On the second Wednesday of the month, right after students are dismissed, the monthly book study on writer's workshop meets in Jen Zimmerman's second-grade classroom. Jen sets out plastic bowls of trail mix and chips in the center of each hexagonal table grouping. Twenty-five kindergarten to second-grade teachers arrive and fill paper plates with goodies before we begin our book study.

Each year, teachers recommend and select a book to purchase, read, and study each month. Reading professional texts during a busy school year can be a challenging discipline. At Moreland Hills, however, we value the social and professional camaraderie of sharing and dissecting these books.

This year's selection was a set of nine books that make up Lucy Calkins's *Units of Study for Primary Writing* (2003a). Talk about a daunting task. A small group of teachers had dabbled in Lucy's approach to writer's workshop during the previous year, and their excitement persuaded us all to give it a go.

We agree to study one book a month to build familiarity with the whole set during the school year. We apply the "jigsaw strategy" of assigning portions of the text to groups of three or four teachers. Between sessions, everyone reads the introduction of the focus text and his or her assigned sections. The groups become our experts, describing key elements and important points. As the year progresses, we marvel at how instructional language can influence writers to explore and to take risks.

Shared Inquiry

In September, I invite classroom teachers or interventionists to participate in individualized mini-research projects called shared inquiries. One to three researchers enroll for two-month spells to participate in self-defined projects. My commitment to the teachers who volunteer is to help frame a question of instructional implementation specific to their interests or classroom needs and to co-design and co-implement a plan for action research in response to the question. I do not participate as the expert and answer-giver. Instead, we work together to discover solutions.

For example, Doreen is a highly skilled fourth-grade teacher with meticulous documentation of each student's reading based on reading conferences, guided reading conversations, and various readers' responses. She volunteered to participate in shared inquiry because she wanted teacher input in determining effective ways of translating notes from six different sources into weekly reading goals and a report card grade. Doreen's query was "What essential observations will inform my instructional decisions?"

Over the course of a month, the two of us examined the hurdles of her current system of record-keeping, reviewed and clarified state indicators and grade-level expectations, and watched for evidence of essential reading behaviors demonstrated in guided reading groups and readers' response journals. We experimented with a few different systems of documentation and finally came up with one manageable sheet per student to record observations and key information.

A small group of kindergarten teachers requested shared inquiry to develop ideas for what meaningful literacy work kindergarten students could do while the teacher facilitated small-group instruction. Together, we framed the question, "What independent literacy tasks might engage kindergarten learners?" We spent a week observing what naturally fascinated kindergartners. We observed that independent playtime and interactive conversations of five-year-olds revealed opportunities for students to create signs, make menus, mark nonfiction picture books with question marks on sticky notes, and on and on.

Shared inquiry emerges from professional self-evaluation and offers opportunities for custom-made problem-solving and study. Its intent is to provide a professional development venue, nestled into the context of everyday workings at our school, that invites veteran teachers to delve more deeply, refine implementation logistics, and improve delivery of instruction. Through shared inquiry, literacy leaders can differentiate support spanning management issues to instructional delivery and from reading to writing while addressing a range of teacher needs.

Classroom Coaching

A powerful way to motivate and sustain change is by demonstrating the cultural expectation. Using the gradual release of responsibility principle (Pearson and Gallagher 1983), classroom coaching flows from direct demonstration through guided practice and ends with a teacher's independent application. Its purpose is to promote a shared understanding of the school's instructional standards and focus.

At Moreland Hills, classroom coaching is primarily used to introduce a commonly adopted instructional framework, such as writer's workshop, reader's workshop, or developmental word study. This requires deliberate attention to surface logistics as well as developing a heightened awareness of instructional intent. We want our teachers to adeptly observe learning behaviors, differentiate for a range of learners, and use prompting or conferring to bring about strategic thinking. That's a tall order. By scheduling coaching sessions centering on our universal instructional frameworks and foundational knowledge, we can reinforce the common language and the climate for professional learning.

The role of the literacy leader in providing classroom coaching explicitly demonstrates how instructional expectations might look and sound and facilitates guided practice with descriptive and responsive feedback. In this role, literacy leaders need to have extensive knowledge and resources at their fingertips. They need to be able to field questions from teachers (and students) as they arise.

Four categories of professional knowledge provide strong classroom coaching. They are (1) *instructional frameworks*, (2) *instructional techniques*, (3) *instructional language*, and (4) *instructional resources*. It is important to understand the intent behind each of these components:

1. Instructional frameworks

* Setting up the environment and routines

* Scheduling instructional blocks

* Progression and pacing of lessons and lesson focus

* Negotiable and nonnegotiable aspects

2. Instructional techniques

* Presenting explicit mini-lessons

* Differentiating small-group instruction

* Evoking thoughtful literacy before, during, and after reading

* Managing routines of meaningful literacy experiences

* Offering descriptive feedback in student conferences

3. Instructional language that facilitates learning

* Language that invites inquiry and risk-taking

* Language that connects to previous learning

* Language that prompts strategic problem-solving

* Language that specifically names the learner's strengths

* Language that clearly names the learning objective and expectation

4. Instructional resources

* Mentor texts

* Professional sources containing further explanations and resources

* Graphic organizers that stimulate discussion

* Alternative accommodations for a range of learners

* Documentation formats

At the beginning of Kari's first year as a first-grade teacher, she was faced with a steep learning curve to assimilate all the procedures and policies of a new school. Added to that was the school's expectation that she learn the processes of guided reading and writer's workshop. Alongside that high expectation was a design for intensive support to yield success. Late in September, after the fall assessments and a classroom community had been established, we reviewed her guided reading groups and set goals for their instruction.

We phased in each reading group as I demonstrated reading group lessons (three or more days per group) that shifted in emphasis according to each stage of readers. Kari studied teacher and students and jotted down questions about their interactions. Later, Kari and I discussed what she observed, and we planned how she might implement the next set of lessons. This time, I observed, not as an evaluator but as an assessor, one who could specify her command of instructional techniques and address misconceptions. In less than a month, Kari presented guided reading with poise. She responded to parent questions with complete and professional assurance.

Training Sessions

Some aspects of professional development need to be addressed directly to sustain instructional and assessment norms. Training sessions could be as brief as an hour (as in practice for taking a running record) or as much as a few days (as in the initial overview of literacy assessments and instructional framework). Professional development might occur in the summer months or during the school year. Nonetheless, training sessions are designed to attend to primary business.

If there is an element of your course of study that is required, you owe it to your teachers to train them in the logistics and rationale. It's been said that teaching is the only profession in which a novice is expected to perform as well as a veteran. The playing field can be leveled for new teachers with a thorough orientation to the resources and instruction procedures beginning on day one.

We routinely provide training sessions for our language arts assessment system, an overview of the reading workshop and writing workshop models, and on the developmental word study approach. Because these differ in delivery according to grade level, we may schedule separate sessions for primary and intermediate grades.

When we want to introduce a new initiative, we lure teachers to attend summer workshops by promising participants incentives such as whiteboards, magnetic letters, and professional texts as gestures of appreciation. (We have to work within the confines of the teacher contract.)

It is crucial to the success of new teachers and their students that we immerse them in the common language with which to enter into our culture as contributing members. Otherwise, we run the risk of losing them to frustration and defeat.

Core Professional Resources

Every classroom in our building holds a collection of professional texts that we recognize as core resources. The teachers are expected to refer to these texts as they design lessons or troubleshoot for student accommodations.

In the past, we had the teacher's edition of the adopted basal series or phonics books as classroom resources. Now, each teacher is equipped with the professional resources that support the school's philosophy and shape lesson planning. Rather than expecting compliant teachers to refer to a scripted series of lessons, we count on our faculty to use professional discretion and expertise. The core professional resources are not a set of books located on a remote shelf in the staff book room but a set of books written by recognized literacy experts and purchased for every teacher's classroom. We refer to them in professional development workshops and they serve as essential instructional supports.

Core professional texts at Moreland Hills are listed in Appendix A.

Site Visits

Viewing the logistics of implementation and listening in on the instructional language of the classroom transforms theory into reality. A workshop leader can talk for hours or we can all read texts on implementing guided reading, but seeing is believing. A site visit is enhanced threefold when teachers reflect on their observations afterward.

It is ideal to find nearby schools in which the instructional framework is in place. I connect with the literacy coordinator or administrator in a neighboring school and arrange for a small group of our teachers to spend two hours observing three or four classrooms during reading and writing instruction. We arrive with notepads and pens. We use maps indicating which classrooms we will visit.

We usually set up an observation with a specific purpose in mind. We might watch for what constitutes independent work while small groups are being facilitated. Or we might look for how the culture reinforces clear expectations. Listening for teacher talk that encourages strategic thinking and draws out rich discussion could also be the emphasis of the day. By setting a specific purpose before the observation, you can focus the discussion afterward to address ingrained misconceptions or to identify applications that refresh or improve practice.

Sharing insights about what we observed during the site visit deepens the understanding of implementation or of the purpose behind an instructional component and provides opportunities to clarify questions. It should not matter whether the setting and language were ideal. Observations that raise awareness of alternative ways a teacher could have responded to an observed classroom situation can be a catalyst for professional reflection on best practices.

Site visits can take on many forms. Arrange to take a teacher's class while he or she observes a classroom down the hall. Schedule to watch a video of master teachers like Debbie Miller (2002) or Stephanie Harvey (2004) providing lessons for young readers, or watch a video recording of a lesson taught at your school. Visit classrooms in another district. What matters is taking the time to observe, to critique, and to raise the level of awareness of professional practice. The aim is to determine what words and actions make a difference for kids.

Professional Release Days

Now and then, you need to provide an "intermission" from the busy routines in the classrooms for teachers to delve into one specific topic without interruption or distraction. Professional release days (releasing teachers for either a half or a full day) help regenerate professional attention to common priorities of instruction and stimulate shared ownership of curricular decisions.

Substitute teachers may be assigned to a third-grade classroom in the morning and then switch to a second-grade classroom in the afternoon to enable certain grade-level groups to participate in a targeted aspect of professional development.

Sometimes the purpose is to study and reach consensus. We might be reviewing state indicators and synthesizing a list of pressing concepts or hearing our teachers for gifted enrichment present ways to differentiate for high-level readers.

Other times, we might spend time developing an important resource in response to what teachers or students need to be more successful: refining grade-level rubrics or designing guided reading lessons that emphasize practicing strategies over teaching the contents of a book.

Whenever our administrators want teachers to acquire specific professional concept knowledge, they provide time for grade-level groupings to attend half-day or whole-day structured instructional investigation. Two or three professional release days per year for each grade level unify and focus the grade-level team.

A full day is scheduled for professional release time on content-area reading. Our fourth- and fifth-grade teachers meet in our large conference room during the morning while substitute teachers take over classes. Stacks of texts, graphic organizers, and an agenda line the center of a long table. The overhead projector is centrally positioned.

Marnie brings homemade crumb cake to share. Our focus is to construct common knowledge of key instructional strategies and practices to support comprehension and reading in science and social studies.

At the beginning, I state the intent of the session, so that our short time together can be used efficiently and effectively: "In these three hours, we'll look at some of the obstacles to reaching and teaching a wide range of readers in your science and social studies instruction. Then we'll explore tools and techniques to make content-area reading more accessible and memorable for all your students. I hope you will each come away with a plan for using specific tools in your content area."

Jackie describes the frustration of having a student who barely speaks English, five kids who cannot read the social studies textbook, and three who answer every question before the study unit begins. We all connect to the common plight of planning for diverse student needs while having to cover so much content in so little time. We generate a list of barriers to addressing the needs of diverse learners.

Articles and excerpts from professional texts help reveal new instructional strategies. I demonstrate techniques for presenting and sorting vocabulary to build familiarity and to organize connections among important terminology. I model one way to apply the technique of story impressions to motivate anticipation for an upcoming unit on explorers. We divide the group to read and share directions for three more instructional strategies that deepen background knowledge and engage student interest. For the final hour of our release time, teachers work in pairs integrating two or three new strategies for increasing motivation and critical thinking in established units of study. After lunch, fourth-grade teachers attend a similar professional development focus.

Consider these options as professional development à la carte. An effective array of professional development runs the gamut from simple to sophisticated. The menu of venues can be used as a comprehensive collection of opportunities, or simply to augment what is already working in your school. I recommend starting with only one or two items, then gradually adding more options as schedules, personnel, and resources become available.

Continuous professional development is a vital component of synchronizing a comprehensive literacy system. The bottom line is this: if schools are committed to mentoring students in becoming lifelong learners, we need to routinely mentor our teachers by regularly providing opportunities for professional and collaborative reflection, for rigorous study of the finest tools of the profession, and for observing and designing high-quality instruction.

What Can Administrators and School Leaders Do?

INCREASE CONTINUITY. *WHAT RESOURCES AND PRACTICES CAN BE MADE MORE CONSISTENT TO ADVANCE THE GOALS OF YOUR COMPREHENSIVE LITERACY SYSTEM?*

* Introduce a culture and expectation for professional reflection, solution-oriented dialogue, site visits, and exchange of ideas and resources.

* Establish monthly routines for professional learning and reflection.

* Develop a five-year plan for gradually phasing in a particular focus/venue of professional development each year.

DEEPEN PROFESSIONAL LEARNING. *HOW CAN YOU SUPPORT THE COMPREHENSIVE LITERACY GOALS WITH ONGOING PROFESSIONAL DEVELOPMENT?*

* Find opportunities to switch the focus from problems to solutions.

* Motivate participation with topics or issues directly relevant to your staff.

* Construct common background knowledge and trust through whole-staff article or book studies and discussion groups.

* Join together diverse role groups in fresh combinations.

* Share thought-provoking education headlines, research summaries, or data as catalysts to spark (and practice) respectful professional dialogue.

EMPOWER COLLABORATIVE LEADERSHIP. *WHAT OPPORTUNITIES FOR COLLABORATIVE LEADERSHIP WILL EXPAND PARTICIPATION AND ADVANCE THE GOALS OF YOUR COMPREHENSIVE LITERACY SYSTEM?*

* Form discussion groups and rotate roles of facilitator, scribe, spokesperson, and timekeeper.

* Note sources of natural leaders, who listen and paraphrase well, for future leadership roles.

* Invite voluntary participation in follow-up groups to carry the group's ideas to fruition with simple action plans. Build momentum with shared ownership and timely resources.

* Encourage teachers to present at state and national conferences.

REALLOCATE RESOURCES. *HOW CAN YOU USE ASSETS YOU ALREADY HAVE IN A WAY THAT WILL ADVANCE THE GOALS OF A COMPREHENSIVE LITERACY SYSTEM?*

* Designate a room in the building or district to set up for professional development sessions.

* Budget or write grants for professional texts, guest speakers, consultants.

* Use ten minutes from the staff meeting agendas for professional development moments, such as modeling instructional techniques and generating lists of questions, issues, or solutions. Ask different staff members to present brief "commercials" highlighting the universal application of an instruction strategy. Use your staff as a think tank to provide continuous feedback and a community of proactive problem-solvers.

* Gradually develop and reassign the role of a reading teacher to serve as an on-site literacy leader for professional development in reading and writing.

Making It Your Own: Reflections for a Custom Fit

A. What do you want your faculty to know and be able to do regarding a culture of professional learning?

B. What specific supports will your faculty need in order to practice professional reflection and study?

C. What assets and resources are available to coordinate the supports necessary?		
Space for Professional Development	Time for Professional Development	Expertise
Models to Observe	Professional References	Core Interest Group

D. Think Big, Start Small: Four Simple Steps Forward

Begin embedding professional development into everyday routines.

1. Create a "spotlight on best practices" in a monthly newsletter to the staff or at intermittent staff meetings.

2. Convene a core team of teachers interested in studying a common topic or issue.

3. Distribute professional response journals to all staff members. Pose a monthly question for professional self-reflection. Create routine opportunities to discuss insights on the topic.

4. Select a monthly article on a topic of interest in education. Place a stack in the teachers' lounge with an open invitation to join a monthly discussion on the article.

6 — Apples to Apples
The Power of Common Assessments

Common FORMATIVE AND SUMMATIVE ASSESSMENTS MAY BE
IDENTICAL TO INDIVIDUAL CLASSROOM FORMATIVE AND SUMMATIVE
ASSESSMENTS EXCEPT FOR ONE NOTABLE DISTINCTION—THEY ARE
DEVELOPED *collaboratively* IN GRADE-LEVEL AND DEPARTMENT TEAMS
AND INCORPORATE EACH TEAM'S COLLECTIVE WISDOM (PROFESSIONAL
KNOWLEDGE AND EXPERIENCE) IN DETERMINING THE SELECTION,
DESIGN, AND ADMINISTRATION OF THOSE ASSESSMENTS.
—*Larry Ainsworth and Donald Viegut,* **Common Formative Assessments:
How to Connect Standards-Based Instruction and Assessment**

Euros: A Common Currency

In 2002, twelve European countries activated a bold innovation to create a common currency: the euro. Before that time, travel between independent European countries required awkward calculations and conversions between the values of lire versus drachma or marks versus francs. When a Spanish merchant named an item's value in terms of pesetas, it was not easy for a visitor to translate that into a more familiar denomination.

The Barriers of Isolation

There was a time at Moreland Hills Elementary School when each classroom teacher and reading specialist used a different form of "currency" as well. A person speaking to one individual classroom teacher and then to another would have to decipher reading progress based on incompatible criteria and terminology. To measure a child's reading level, Linda used standardized passages leveled incrementally, wheras Amy used word lists designed to predict grade level of reading skill. Elaine referred to basal levels, whereas Barb used terms like "instructional" and "independent."

At that time, even the decision whether to assess or document student progress had been left entirely to each teacher's discretion (or handed over to the reading specialist). Over many years, that unrestricted freedom of choice evolved into a disarray of rubrics, text-leveling systems, checklists, reading scales, and general hunches. As a result, the widely subjective judgment based on a teacher's gut feeling often determined whether a child was offered supplemental support.

When our practice was so disjointed, we put parents in the awkward position of having to interpret conference reports based on inconsistent contexts and vocabulary. If parents had children in two or more grade levels (as most do), heaven help them! They'd have to operate multiple conversion systems at every parent/teacher conference. We were collectively constructing obstacles against the home-school partnership as well as the efforts of every teacher throughout a child's school career. Students could not receive the full benefit of any instructional efforts because we kept changing the context and standards from room to room and from year to year.

Designing Assessments for a Custom Fit

The force that finally propelled our staff onto a mutual path toward continuity was not a mandate from above but a joint decision to develop universal assessments. We realized that it was counterproductive to have so many incoherent ways for describing student achievement. We had each applied different criteria and used a separate vocabulary to judge literacy behaviors, virtually comparing yardsticks to liters. Were we speaking the same language? Desperate for some mutual way of describing how students were progressing in reading and writing, we wanted a system for comparing apples to apples.

As soon as we began the cooperative process of selecting, designing, and administering common literacy assessments, we discovered the power of a shared language and a united frame of reference. We shifted from individual currencies for valuing student progress to a common "euro" of consistent communication.

To coordinate a plan of action, a literacy team was formed, with representative voices from all the players:

* Two classroom teachers from each grade, preschool through grade five

* An administrator

* Two special education teachers

* Reading specialists

The aim of the team was to work together to increase the continuity of literacy support for students across the grade levels. In its first year, members of the literacy team took on the challenge of replacing our splintered assessment practices with a common set of measurements to administer in classrooms every fall and spring.

From the start of our process for developing an assessment system, we did not intend to purchase commercially made assessment kits to solve all our woes. The kits were alarmingly pricey, and they all contained pieces and parts we did not want. What's more, we saw value in collaboratively designing a custom fit of assessment choices to our own setting, something we owned and shared with mutual commitment. The time and effort would truly be worthwhile if, as a result, classroom teachers could gather practical data that directly applied to supporting students in reading and writing.

First of all, we needed to get a sense of the possibilities:

* What informal assessments were readily available?

* What skills did each one assess?

* What assessment solutions were being used in other districts?

* How could assessment results be organized in a meaningful and usable format?

Where to begin? At the onset, we surveyed our colleagues to shed light on what information they would find valuable to know and track concerning young readers and writers. It became critical, too, for the group to agree on the difference between "interesting to know about a student" and "important to designing classroom instruction." The idea of developing common classroom assessments certainly did not mean transplanting the detailed diagnostics of a reading specialist into a classroom setting. Those kinds of detailed examinations could be left to the specialists when classroom assessment scores indicated a need for more intensive supplemental support and targeted goals. Instead, classroom teachers needed assessments that were user-friendly to students and teachers: manageable logistics along with the kind of information immediately applicable to helping clusters of children gain specific strategies or skills (see Figure 6.1). As part of the selection process, teachers used some assessments with their students to evaluate the format and ease of manageability.

6.1 Linking Literacy Skills Assessed to Classroom Action

LITERACY SKILLS ASSESSED	CLASSROOM ACTION (RESPONDING TO LOW PERFORMANCE USING ASSESSMENT RESULTS)
Concepts of print; general book knowledge	Explicitly model and provide practice using book terminology and concepts to small groups or whole group ("first"/"last," "word"/"letter," 1:1 pointing to words, naming punctuation, locating words embedded in text based on the first sound)
Rhyming	Model and provide practice playing with oral rhyming
Letter identification	Model and provide practice of letter formation, naming letters, identifying letter features, sorting, pairing capitals to lowercase
Hearing and recording sounds in words	Model and provide practice labeling pictures and items Practice stretching words with slow articulation Share and scaffold the recording task Play sound-symbol association tasks
Strategic performance on incremental reading levels	Create homogeneous groupings based on needs for strategy instruction and developmental reading stage
Comprehension	Explicitly demonstrate and practice applying comprehension strategies Weigh the balance of need for literal vs. inferential comprehension strategy instruction
Oral reading accuracy (from a selected passage)	Explicitly demonstrate and provide practice applying neglected fix-up strategies Increase opportunities for independent reading within an appropriate range of levels
Rate of self-correction	Increase direct attention and practice to the job of a reader to notice errors and to actively select a fix-up strategy
Reading fluency	Determine whether fluency issue results from difficulty with instant word recognition, expressive intonation, or rate Model and provide practice to the area of fluency needed
Rapid reading of high-utility words in isolation	Target a specific set of high-frequency words to master at a time Provide frequent opportunities to locate, sort, or identify specific high-frequency words
Developmental spelling stage	Focus accountability for spelling application within the student's stage of development Provide explicit instruction within each student's stage Provide strategic word wall practice within developmental stage of the majority of students

Accuracy of spelling the grade-level high-frequency words	Use words to link to new concepts of spelling or word analysis
Independent application of writing conventions	Determine priorities for whole-group instruction vs. small-group instruction based on mastery in the classroom
Interest inventory	Link student work to areas of interest where possible

Once we knew generally what we were looking for, we sent the grade-level representatives and reading specialists into the hinterlands to gather examples of assessments of reading and writing. They queried colleagues from other districts, shared examples of assessments used, and looked up informal assessments referenced in university courses. They found an assortment of leveled reading passages and word lists, skill checklists, and rubrics describing varying degrees of student performance. There were some minutely-detailed continuums of developmental progressions as well as the "quick and easy" variety of assessments promising to calculate an accurate reading level, identify students at risk, and basically reorganize your whole filing system in just five minutes. We reviewed them all. The process and discussions helped us draw a collective picture of what features we regarded as relevant and reasonable for classroom use. Figures 6.2 and 6.3 show the format we used to organize our critiques of the many assessments we analyzed. Appendix B contains blank forms that you can use.

Figure 6.2 Critique of Reading Assessments

Assessment	For Which Grade Level(s)?	State Reading Indicators Assessed	User-Friendly for Kids?	User-Friendly for Classroom Teachers?	Training Needed for Standardized Administration	Comments

Figure 6.3 Critique of Writing Assessments

Assessment	For Which Grade Level(s)?	State Writing Indicators Assessed	User-Friendly for Kids?	User-Friendly for Classroom Teachers?	Training Needed for Standardized Administration	Comments

Selecting and organizing our own set of assessments was a messy process. It was not as simple and neat as breaking through the cellophane of a ready-made set of materials and distributing them in pretty plastic totes. Some days we wondered, will it ever get off the ground? As a literacy leader, I facilitated collegial conversations through a sequence of steps (see the chart "Developing Common Literacy Assessments" in Figure 6.4) to create an assessment system tailored to what we, as professionals, recognized as valuable. At times, we got bogged down in semantics or buried in the details of collating pages for resource notebooks.

I focused on our principal's steady mantra: "Patience, Maren. Baby steps." And, finally, it was launched! The two-year process shifted through phases from studying options and alternatives, to establishing consensus on the selection criteria at each grade level, culminating with grade-specific notebooks filled with the instructions and protocols necessary for piloting the assessments in the fall for preschool through fifth grade.

The staff's commitment to invest energy in these new assessment routines rested on the success of our pilot year. Because of the steep learning curve for all of us, our principal offered release days for training sessions and extra support to make individual assessment manageable to classroom teachers. Reading specialists and special education teachers pitched in to help administer some of the assessments or to provide whole-class activities and free up the classroom teacher to administer assessments to individual students. By easing the burden for each other, support staff sent out a hopeful message: We are all in this together.

Feedback from our classroom teachers confirmed that the hours of critiquing and collating materials had paid off. Teachers reported that, although the process required more work, the information gained about individual students as well as our own increased ability to compare student growth using a common literacy language was worth the added effort. Ownership created surprising momentum. Administrators and teachers appreciated "speaking the same language" in parent conferences or professional meetings when they were describing student performance.

We continue to refine and review the assessment system each school year. And it just gets better and better. The assessments serve as a classroom formative assessment in the fall, as teachers observe reading behaviors and use the assessments to prioritize instructional goals and tailor lessons to meet the needs of their students. Then, in the spring, test scores provide summative documentation of end-of-year levels achieved. In an era pressured with mandates from the *No Child Left Behind Act* and state demands for data demonstrating student gains, districts are pressured to race for the assessment package gleaming with the most sparkle and promise. I will tell you plainly that the process of engaging in professional conversation and study to develop an assessment system we can call our own holds value well beyond a prepackaged decoy. A patient and shared process benefits students and teachers tenfold.

The creation of the Language Arts Assessment System (LAAS) generated enthusiasm and caused a rush of other unifying possibilities to follow. Teachers called for an accessible database of student scores and for a literacy portfolio to travel with children from one grade level to the next. The literacy team became the energizing thrust pushing our Moreland Hills literacy reforms, initiated with the voice of our teachers. For a list of our selected literacy assessments, see Figure 6.5.

6.4 Developing Common Literacy Assessments

STEP	ACTION	MATERIALS NEEDED
1	In grade-level groups, list the kind of information that is most useful and practical to provide quality literacy support in the classroom. (Consider suggestions per grade level for fall and spring.) Share suggestions with whole group, preschool through grade 5.	Chart paper for each group Markers
2	Participants locate samples of assessments for reading, writing, and word study skills: * Checklists * Passages with comprehension questions * Word lists * Rubrics * Other	Samples from colleagues and representatives inside and outside the district
3	Review a wide range of assessments that measure reading and writing across the targeted grade levels. In groups representing primary or intermediate grades, review grade-appropriate assessments. Record comments regarding pros and cons, questions, and ideas generated. Sort assessment samples into piles of "potential" and "unlikely." Share observations with the whole group.	The sample assessments gathered from other districts, commercially made products, other tests used by teachers in the building
4	Use critique forms to evaluate the "potential" assessments.	Critique of writing assessments Critique of reading assessments
5	Propose selected set of common assessments to grade levels for approval.	Samples of selected assessments to distribute at grade-level meetings

| 6 | Determine what resources need to be created or compiled in order for teachers to pilot the selected assessments.

Create a task force to develop the needed pages by a given deadline.

Create assessment system notebooks that include the student copies or passages, teacher copies, directions for administering tests, and directions for scoring tests. | Assessment prep sheets

Notebooks or web resources

Computers

Copyright permission, as needed

Copier or scanner |
| 7 | Aim to pilot common assessments for three grades, fall and spring of the next full school year.

Provide supports and training as needed. Gather feedback from teachers. | Appropriate materials and copies

Time and designed demonstrations for training teachers on assessments

Networked support from reading specialists and special education teachers to assist in the logistics of individual assessment |

6.5 List of Selected Literacy Assessments

SELECTED PRIMARY-GRADE ASSESSMENTS KINDERGARTEN TO THIRD GRADE	SELECTED INTERMEDIATE-GRADE ASSESSMENTS FOURTH AND FIFTH GRADE
Developmental Reading Assessment	Qualitative Reading Inventory
Developmental Spelling Analysis	Developmental Spelling Analysis
Writing to a Prompt	Writing to a Prompt
Word Recognition (Fry Words)	
Writing Grade-Level "Snap Words" (K–3)	
Sentence Dictation for Hearing and Recording Sounds in Words (K and 1)	
Letter Identification (K only)	
Concepts of Print (K only)	

(A description of each of these assessments can be found in Appendix C.)

A Database for Whole-School Reporting

It was Anne who nudged us into the new millennium. In addition to being an extraordinary second-grade teacher, Anne was our staff technology representative. Always on the lookout for opportunities to integrate technology into our professional work, Anne suggested we compile a schoolwide database. That seemed a bit daunting to me. Who was going to enter all those names and all those scores? We have more than 1,000 students in our building!

Amazingly, two volunteer teachers stepped forward (or else all others stepped backward), volunteering to enter data during the summer, once a database was created. With the assistance of our technology department, we designed a user-friendly database. FileMaker Pro software made it simple to access and record individual scores for students from preschool through fifth grade. With the new database, one could view, at a glance, each student's literacy growth and reading support across several grades. A teacher could sort records by classroom group or intervention caseload for any given school year.

One data bank of scores made it possible for reading or enrichment specialists to locate lists of students based on certain performance criteria more efficiently and to begin the process of further observation or assessment for a new year. As a result, supplemental remediation or enrichment groups could begin sooner than in previous years. Classroom teachers could check previous scores to estimate an appropriate level to start each student's assessment. Once fall scores were entered, teachers could immediately sort class lists and establish initial groupings for differentiated instruction in reading and word study.

The literacy team could establish realistic benchmarks for student achievement at each grade level because scores were easy to access. A quality assessment process empowered quality instruction.

Beyond Just the Numbers: The Literacy Portfolio

Once a synchronized assessment system was in place, with fall and spring assessments entered into the database each year, teachers requested a format for sharing samples of student work from grade to grade. We knew that cold scores and statistics did not adequately depict each child's academic progress during the course of a school year. Student samples captured how much a student had advanced in skill and sophistication. Our common assessments provided evidence of a student's progress in writing from fall to spring as well as his or her application of reading strategies for monitoring and self-correction during oral reading. In essence, we wanted hard evidence for subsequent teachers that, although Celeste did not reach the benchmark score, she had traveled from a significant disadvantage to near success. Whatever the motivation, another project for our literacy team was to determine which artifacts to include in a literacy portfolio file created to follow a child from one grade level to the next.

Conversations between grade levels helped us agree on which pieces from the assessments would be worthwhile to preserve and compare across time. Third-grade teachers requested that second grade include recent student work but did not see a reason for keeping kindergarten or first-grade samples in the portfolio. Fifth-grade teachers asked fourth-grade teachers to include a prompted writing sample because the state achievement test did not return the written piece.

Our school secretary set up folders for every child in the building, and the literacy team decided which assessment items to include from preschool to fifth grade. Our principal developed a system for having these literacy portfolios turned in with each student's cumulative file at the end of the school year. The following school year, the portfolios are redistributed in new classroom groupings, ready for added assessment items. Every student moving from our elementary school into the middle school has a literacy portfolio and six years of assessment data. Now the middle school staff wants to know more about our process. The literacy portfolios promoted continuity and contributed another unifying element of collective intent.

Refine, Refine, Refine

The Language Arts Assessment System now holds eight years of data. Every child has a portfolio that celebrates progress and goals, and a database of each student's literacy progression from preschool through fifth grade can be found on every teacher's computer desktop. Yet, we continue to refine our original work.

Because we value one another's feedback, we continue to make small adjustments to our work. For the first few years, our second-grade teachers administered a sentence dictation task, but teachers decided the information gained duplicated the writing competency task. Originally, we used an assessment tool for determining reading level based on grade-leveled word recognition lists. Experience taught us that we could make better assessment/instruction connections by checking recognition of high-frequency words instead of grade-leveled word lists. Student errors in reading high-frequency words could directly apply to classroom instruction to increase automatic word recognition and students could even graph their own progress.

I may be paranoid, but I believe that technology department staff sometimes resist my calls because they know I will ask them to add a field to the database or recommend a new screen arrangement that increases usability for interventionists, administrators, or classroom teachers. They're right. I will.

Eight years of success, and we are still refining the system. I don't expect the refinements to reach perfection (we might be on version 7.0 by now). There will always be room for improvement, and I hope Moreland Hills teachers, staff, and administrators will remain open to working on the cutting edge of quality educational practice. The journey reaps as much reward as the destination. Our professional acuity and respect for one another have been raised to new heights.

Now, more than sixty teachers and administrators routinely use the same terms for measuring reading and writing. Now, we all easily access vital information that can increase our collective ability to respond proactively to specific needs of students. We are fluent in the same literacy language, and the result is observable and measurable growth for our kids. Mike Schmoker describes this in *Results: The Key to Continuous School Improvement* (1996):

> *If leadership provided the encouragement and opportunity for practitioners to begin gathering and examining collective student results, we would make real strides toward understanding our strengths and weaknesses.... Group data maximize our ability to develop the most effective improvement and corrective action and to focus that action on the highest priority areas, those with the greatest opportunity for improvement. (43)*

What Can Administrators and School Leaders Do?

INCREASE CONTINUITY. *WHAT RESOURCES AND PRACTICES CAN BE MADE MORE CONSISTENT TO ADVANCE THE GOALS OF YOUR COMPREHENSIVE LITERACY SYSTEM?*

* Develop a plan for gradually phasing in a particular piece of common assessment each year.

* Communicate timelines expected for assessment and deadlines for documentation or data entry.

DEEPEN PROFESSIONAL LEARNING. *HOW CAN WE SUPPORT THE COMPREHENSIVE LITERACY GOALS WITH ONGOING PROFESSIONAL DEVELOPMENT?*

* Locate a variety of sample assessment materials used in your classrooms, in other districts, or promoted by education companies. Facilitate assessment critiques by collaborative teams.

* Participate in the discussions and critiques regarding helpful reader information, logistical implications of assessments, and final assessment selection.

* Provide for training in administering assessments and documenting results.

* Facilitate opportunities for teachers to practice reviewing sample assessment results in ways that drive instructional decisions.

EMPOWER COLLABORATIVE LEADERSHIP. *WHAT OPPORTUNITIES FOR COLLABORATIVE LEADERSHIP WILL EXPAND PARTICIPATION AND ADVANCE THE GOALS OF YOUR COMPREHENSIVE LITERACY SYSTEM?*

* Invite all teachers to contribute assessments to consider.

*Ask grade-level teams to list the student data they would want to measure and use and how often it should be measured or used.

*Organize literacy team representatives to initiate a monthly feedback cycle between the literacy team and represented constituencies throughout the process of assessment selection, design, piloting, and logistics.

* Empower collaborative teams to develop notebooks or web pages of materials teachers will need for assessment.

* Encourage the literacy team to determine which pieces to add to a student's literacy portfolio each year.

REALLOCATE RESOURCES. *HOW CAN YOU USE ASSETS YOU ALREADY HAVE IN A WAY THAT WILL ADVANCE THE GOALS OF A COMPREHENSIVE LITERACY SYSTEM?*

* Designate a storage place for materials as needed.

* Identify technological support staff for setting up a user-friendly database of assessment scores, posting assessment protocols in a shared file, or generating timely data reports.

* Allocate funds for purchase of the necessary assessment materials.

* When launching classroom assessments, support manageability by either providing teachers with release time or with substitute teachers to teach classes while the classroom teacher works with individual students. Administrators or academic support staff might also supervise whole-class lessons to free the classroom teacher for assessment.

Making It Your Own: Reflections for a Custom Fit

A. What assessment practices do you want your faculty to know and be able to do?

B. What specific supports will your faculty need in order to implement customary common assessments and use common measurement criteria?

C. What assets and resources are available to coordinate the supports necessary?		
Space for Professional Development	Time for Professional Development	Expertise
Models to Observe	Professional References	Core Interest Group

D. *Think Big, Start Small: Four Simple Steps Forward*

1. Pilot one common assessment in a small range of grades. Start with a simple assessment that provides helpful information and is easy to administer (such as a checklist or rubric correlated to reading fluency, word recognition, or writing conventions).

2. Invite a core interest group to pilot an assessment and offer feedback.

3. Interview teachers and administrators from a district already employing a common assessment system. Find out what works well and what remains challenging.

4. Motivate informal classroom research to discover observable literacy behaviors. What behaviors tend to indicate strengths in reading or writing?

7 – Standing on Strong Shoulders

THE CHILDREN IN OUR CLASSROOMS NEED US TO WORK TOGETHER
AS A TEAM TO SUPPORT THEM ON THEIR PATHWAY TO LITERACY.
SYSTEMIC CHANGE LIES IN OUR UNDERSTANDING HOW OUR CHILDREN
LEARN AND IN OUR ABILITY TO PROBLEM-SOLVE WITH COLLEAGUES
WHO WORK WITH OUR CHILDREN, WHO SHARE OUR COMMON
EXPERIENCES, AND WHO SPEAK OUR LANGUAGE OF LITERACY.
—*Linda Dorn, Cathy French, and Tammy Jones* Apprenticeship in
Literacy: Transitions Across Reading and Writing

On any given morning, you can walk through the halls of Moreland Hills Elementary School and overhear the murmur of student activity unique to each classroom. Peek inside a few rooms and you will see and hear learning environments set up and managed very differently from one another. Yet, consistent instructional standards link one to another.

A vibrant buzz of student voices spills out of one fourth-grade classroom. An enthusiastic cluster of students practice reader's theater in preparation for the second-grade audience they will visit on Friday. Meanwhile several students lounge comfortably around the room: some are nestled in beanbag chairs or on pillows, two kids are stretched belly-down on the carpet with books or magazines, still others work in pairs to compose character descriptions on laptop computers. Amid the constant flow of motion, the teacher calls individual students to the reading table to conduct brief reading conferences. She records observations in a thick tabbed binder.

Down the hall, another fourth-grade classroom conveys a contrasting ambience. Most students are seated at desks, set in an orderly horseshoe configuration, facing the whiteboard. An overhead projector rests on a cart beside a tall wooden stool. Colorful bins classify books by genre, series, or author names arranged in neat rows along low shelves. The walls exhibit neatly printed posters reminding students of how to select "just right" books or delineating the key elements to include in a journal response to literature. Some students quietly fill in graphic organizers designed to serve as catalysts for small-group discussions about texts read, while others are engrossed in self-selected reading. Meanwhile, the teacher calmly convenes a guided reading group at a corner table for discussion about a story they are reading.

While some teachers are more comfortable facilitating a quiet, methodical learning environment, other teachers are at ease orchestrating students' work in dynamic activity. Students differ from one another and so do teachers, and differing styles can accomplish equal levels of profound learning.

Consistent instruction does not mean that every classroom has to operate uniformly. Such tedium would be demeaning to both teachers and students. Students deserve talented, dedicated, and knowledgeable teachers; and teaching merits the respect of professional autonomy. In the process of increasing instructional continuity, we don't want to diminish professional acumen by creating a dependence on instructional scripts or rules for identical environments. The question becomes, What aspects of instructional continuity will propagate student learning? If students are to become critical thinkers, their teachers need to engage in critical thinking about student learning. Therefore, schools need to draw the lines of continuity in places that honor both the teaching and the learning.

What instructional alignment can do is enable the academic systems of support to integrate more efficiently, effectively, and economically. Together, the school faculty can focus on implementing clear and common standards for quality instruction. Teachers and administrators can explore common professional development topics, integrate intervention models with classroom priorities, and coordinate a shared collection of resources. The instructional alignment also enables students each year to build on reliable foundational blocks of familiarity, accountability, and confidence. Children need us to coordinate our efforts and construct the kind of continuity that sets up conditions for their success. Instructional alignment empowers students with the following:

* *Familiarity*—The student's connections to established schema provide the comfortable déjà vu feeling that invites a student to take initiative in his or her own learning.

* *Accountability*—The student's awareness that classroom teachers and interventionists monitor the same set of expectations reinforces the student's self-efficacy.

* *Confidence*—The student's repeated assurance that a united community of concerned adults is committed for the long haul to see the student succeed communicates to the student a pledge of perseverance.

When the game keeps changing on students from year to year or from room to room, we do our students and ourselves a grave disservice. One year a teacher evaluates writing based on conventions of spelling and capitalization but ignores content; the next year's teacher emphasizes craft and postpones editing. These inconsistencies teach kids the "guess what this teacher is thinking" game, and to win, students need to be mind readers and recognize covert signals. We teach them that we value compliance over self-reliance. Unwittingly, we unravel the fabric created by the previous year's teaching and learning whenever we switch the expectations or contradict the message emphasized by previous or parallel instruction. Instead, wouldn't it make sense to draw together common threads so that students easily recognize the concept-tapestry as it unfolds from year to year?

"Quality Instruction"

Over the course of ten years, four component themes have helped our Moreland Hills Elementary School community standardize quality instruction across six grade levels and build continuity without compromising individual styles of delivery:

1. Implementing common instructional frameworks
2. Defining quality instruction
3. Integrating intervention with classroom systems
4. Prioritizing the curriculum

Refining each component theme continues to drive building-wide improvements, with a little fine-tuning each year. The sequence of facilitating each of these themes hasn't appeared to matter as much as expanding the commitment and ownership across forty-six classrooms, several intervention delivery models, and administrative backing. A phase-in plan of four or five years ensures greater success than any attempt at a comprehensive launch. Patience pays off. The process builds unification and momentum. When the multiple constituents of teachers, parents, and administrators form a unified pyramid to support student learning, our children are raised up on the strong shoulders of an integrated system.

Implementing Common Instructional Frameworks

What Is an Instructional Framework?

Routine lesson components and basic beliefs that frame instructional emphasis and design make up an instructional framework. Some popular examples of instructional frameworks for reading and writing that correspond strongly to evidence-based practice include recipro-cal teaching, reading workshop, balanced literacy, 6+1 Trait Writing, writing workshop, and developmental word study. Developing common instructional frameworks within and across grade levels creates familiar anchors of routine, cognitive strategies, and instructional language that students and teachers can build on with greater levels of sophistication.

When the basic instructional framework remains constant each year, students recognize the lay of the land and can readily connect known concepts to new concepts. Students transition into new classrooms or new units of study with more self-reliance because aspects of the routine or lesson references straightforwardly tie to previous experiences. A new year with a new teacher means being guided into familiar, yet deeper, territory. Establishing common instructional frameworks between grade levels helps orient learning and facilitates a common set of reference points.

Similar instructional frameworks open countless advantages across a school community. Teachers can collaborate on lesson design and share instructional materials such as mini-lessons, collections of mentor texts, or concept sorts. Professional development topics can be tied to a focus and to practical implementation based on a common instructional language or aspects of a lesson. Budgets can be consolidated to finance core professional texts, shared instructional resources, and initiatives specifically related to the universal framework. Parents can build a knowledge base of essential ideas, such as comprehension strategies or nonfiction text structures, that can be generalized across any developmental age to encourage understand-ing and motivation at any grade level. Figure 7.1 lists benefits to various role groups when establishing common instructional frameworks across multiple grade levels.

At Moreland Hills, teachers implement three common instructional frameworks: (1) reading workshop (Fountas and Pinnell 1996, 2001; Calkins 2001), (2) writing workshop (Anderson 2000; Atwell 2002; Calkins 2003a; Graves 1994), and (3) developmental word study approach (Bear et al. 2000; Ganske 2000) in all classrooms from kindergarten through fifth grade. These frameworks are flexibly applied across a range of learners and stages of development and promote conditions of high-quality instruction. They also mutually represent constructivist approaches grounded in evidence-based practice, including

* explicit strategy instruction;

* use of dynamic and differentiated grouping;

* routines of ongoing assessments and descriptive feedback;

* a balance of personal relevance and rigor for each student.

Figure 7.1 Benefits of Common Instructional Frameworks to Various Constituents

CONSTITUENTS	BENEFITS OF ESTABLISHING COMMON INSTRUCTIONAL FRAMEWORKS
Students	Familiarity with lesson elements and expectations
	Instruction connects to established schema of concepts and skills
	Less time spent on review during transitions
	A common instructional language supports focus on content rather than on translating from previous instruction; less confusion
Teachers	Climate expectations are established sooner because of similarity
	Able to refer to and build on "anchor lessons" from previous years
	Common language facilitates dialogue among colleagues
	Common criteria and framework sets common ground for critiquing lesson design and/or student work
	Facilitates collaborative resource exchange and development
	Defines and refines professional philosophy and values
Parents	Builds parent's familiarity with instructional expectations and intent
	Common language over multiple years includes parents in the educational conversation
	Increases parent's capability to know how to offer home support
	Increases confidence in a system that is integrated and focused
School Leaders	Helps define "quality" in practical terms
	Focuses design for professional development
	Facilitates common benchmarks/criteria for student achievement
	Consolidates budget toward related resources
	Provides observable and measurable instructional elements

Appendix D lists references that further describe and support these frameworks.

Although our teachers use different management formats, such as learning stations, mini-research projects, or independent reading routines for their scheduled literacy block, all grade levels of students in reading workshop can count on whole-group mini-lessons explicitly demonstrating strategic thinking, regular small reading groups, and responsive conversations that invite readers to discuss confusions, connections, and insights around a text. Students, progressing from kindergarten through fifth grade in writing workshop, can rely on each teacher's expectation for them to generate a collection of personal topics and to recognize what is meant by zooming in on a small moment or seeing the world through a "poet's eyes" (Calkins 2003a). A child's progression through a series of developmentally sequenced word study features builds and accelerates seamlessly from one year to the next, with watchful teachers monitoring growth or gaps in application based on a common continuum of stages and indicators.

Lucy Calkins describes the economy achieved by capitalizing on students' and teachers' efforts in this way: "When teachers across a grade level agree to travel in synchronicity, they are able to plan and reflect collaboratively. Grade level meetings can become a time for teachers to swap ideas for their minilessons, to wrestle with shared problems, and to function as a curricular support group…. This structure also allows professional development to be aligned with instruction" (Calkins 2003b, 20). So a broader capacity for learning and teaching is launched when instructional frameworks coincide.

Aligning Instructional Frameworks

The process of introducing and adopting each framework into the mainstream of all classrooms has been a gradual one at Moreland Hills—a spiraling rather than a linear progression. Originally, every classroom was an island. We had plenty of individual "star teachers" with noteworthy techniques, monitoring systems, and stimulating lessons. We thought we were doing just fine by most standards: Most of our students were achieving adequately. However, once we realized the payback from applying the common assessment system and consistent criteria to describing students' reading progress, it didn't take long to imagine further advantages, such as extending our newfound continuity into instruction.

Heeding Michael Fullan's advice to "think big, start small," we started unifying one instructional format (reading workshop), a small range of grade levels (kindergarten to second grade), and a group of interested teachers within that range of grades. To whet professional appetites, we invited teachers to study components of reading workshop. We coordinated site visits to neighboring school districts to observe different implementation styles for reading workshop. After each visit, we addressed such questions as

* What was similar to what you already do to instruct reading?

* What was different from what you currently do in reading, yet remarkable? What was remarkable about it?

* What aspects of the environment, instructional focus, language, or routines appeared to be common threads across every classroom visited?

* What evidence of the gradual release of responsibility model (Pearson and Gallagher 1983) was observed?

We also scheduled time to pose questions to some classroom teachers and administrators from the districts we observed (either in person or via email) to fill in the missing pieces of what we observed.

That same year, we directed grant funds to finance a weeklong summer academy focused on guided reading for kindergarten through second grade. We invited an outside educational consultant to demonstrate the framework of reading workshop in the primary grades and to instruct us in designing manageable and literacy-rich environments, taking running records, giving supportive book introductions, prompting for strategic problem-solving, and recognizing a gradient of text characteristics.

By the second year, while teachers who attended the summer academy piloted implementation, we coordinated monthly after-school sessions with guest teachers from some of the schools observed to address topics of specific logistics and application as generated by the faculty. These sessions were open to anyone interested and served to motivate "bystanders" who occasionally popped in to find out what this reading workshop was about. The sessions also offered opportunities to clarify logistical questions for those dabbling in the implementation process. It is important to provide frequent entry points and invitations to build a comfort level with impending change alongside the stated deadlines for expecting full participation.

A chart listing conditions necessary for developing a common instructional framework and possible action steps to facilitate each condition is depicted in Figure 7.2. Instead of waiting for perfect conditions to arrive, launching some part of the framework as "version 1.0" fed the momentum, communicated a tentative trial, informed the next steps, or revealed key resource people.

Whenever a new instructional framework has been introduced, it grows in stages, allowing people to enter the process at various points, with an expected target for full participation about three or four years out. Action steps reveal immediate gains, build momentum with deliberate efforts to increase participation and ownership, and incorporate infrastructures to normalize the framework and sustain continued improvement.

Figure 7.2 Common Instructional Frameworks and Action Steps

CONDITIONS NEEDED	POSSIBLE ACTIONS
Understanding of the Theory and Logistical Framework	Arrange site visits to districts or classrooms implementing the desired framework
	Provide professional reading resources describing the evidence-based theory and practice substantiating the framework implementation
	Coordinate time/money for guest speakers or consultants (including classroom teachers or administrators from districts implementing the framework) and for attendance to related workshops or conferences
	Form a consortium with a nearby district or school to study the framework together
	Empower yearlong study groups to focus on "unpacking" concepts of theory and practice important to the framework
	Provide intensive training for initial implementation
Experiential Application	Invite some teachers to dabble with implementing some components
	Invite those who have studied it to pilot the whole framework
Broad Participation	Open study groups and inservices about the framework to regular attendees as well as for "lurkers" to pop in
	Frequently communicate successes, opportunities, techniques, and open invitations to participate in some aspect of implementation
	Encourage and coordinate additional site visits (either in-house or other districts)
	Offer incentives of resources or supports for participation
	Include parents in the learning
	Propose framework adoption to the board of education
Supports for Implementation	Provide summer academies for intensive training
	Empower collaborative resource development
	Distribute core professional resource texts to all
	Provide monthly forums for troubleshooting and sharing solutions
	Offer classroom demonstration, coaching, and debriefing
	Prepare all new teachers to use the framework
Administrative Expectation	Communicate a timeline for full implementation
	Provide ways to support implementation success
	Participate in some of the study groups and related conferences
	Know what to observe and support in classrooms
	Empower leadership
	Give specific feedback related to the framework during professional evaluations
	Require some professional goals to reflect use of the framework
	Express guidelines defining quality implementation

What Can Administrators and School Leaders Do?

INCREASE CONTINUITY. *WHAT RESOURCES AND PRACTICES CAN BE MADE MORE CONSISTENT TO ADVANCE THE GOALS OF YOUR COMPREHENSIVE LITERACY SYSTEM?*

* Establish parameters for the expected blocks of time and frequency of weekly reading and writing instruction.

* Communicate the evidence-based features of literacy instruction expected.

* Refer to the quality instructional features in instructional guidelines and rubrics, during professional goal setting, and as part of the expectation for professional evaluation.

DEEPEN PROFESSIONAL LEARNING. *HOW CAN YOU SUPPORT THE COMPREHENSIVE LITERACY GOALS WITH ONGOING PROFESSIONAL DEVELOPMENT?*

* Organize site visits and video-viewing of intended instructional frameworks. Set up discussion points with a focus of attention and reflection.

* Provide book study sessions of professional texts organized to describe the logistics and intent of the selected framework.

* Coordinate academy weeks, with incentives of instructional materials, during summer break. Keep a record of resources and future training opportunities the presenter recommends.

EMPOWER COLLABORATIVE LEADERSHIP. *WHAT OPPORTUNITIES FOR COLLABORATIVE LEADERSHIP WILL EXPAND PARTICIPATION AND ADVANCE THE GOALS OF YOUR COMPREHENSIVE LITERACY SYSTEM?*

* Empower a team to organize a collective book room of leveled text sets and professional resources.

* Encourage groups to generate shared resources supporting manageable implementation of the intended framework.

REALLOCATE RESOURCES. *HOW CAN YOU USE ASSETS YOU ALREADY HAVE IN A WAY THAT WILL ADVANCE THE GOALS OF A COMPREHENSIVE LITERACY SYSTEM?*

* Set up a central space (cabinets, shelving, file drawers) to store a community collection of leveled student texts.

* Budget for enhancing classroom library collections for independent reading.

* Fund summer academies to launch training in the instructional frameworks.

Making It Your Own: Reflections for a Custom Fit

A. What instructional practices do you want your faculty to know and be able to do?

B. What specific supports will your faculty need in order to customarily implement the intended instructional features?

C. What assets and resources are available to coordinate the supports necessary?		
Space for Professional Development	Time for Professional Development	Expertise
Models to Observe	Professional References	Core Interest Group

D. Think Big, Start Small: Four Simple Steps Forward

1. Convene a core of interested teachers to study a particular instructional framework.

2. Organize site visits and attendance to conferences or workshops presenting the intended framework, beginning with the core of interested teachers.

3. Instigate interest by inviting teachers implementing the framework in neighborhood schools to present components during short, after-school sessions.

4. Motivate classroom teachers to dabble with implementation of one or two components (perhaps establishing independent reading routines and conferring sessions) and to provide feedback regarding the benefits and challenges.

Defining Quality with Evidence-Based Practices

Establishing a common instructional framework creates a visible structure, at the school and district levels, for readily connecting professional development, instructional language, and resources. Yet a cohesive instructional approach across forty-six classrooms can still fall short of clearly defining "quality instruction" for teachers and administrators.

Directives from the *No Child Left Behind Act* put the pressure on school leaders to scrutinize instruction for evidence-based practice. Of course, the selection of evidence-based practice is easier said than done. School leaders have to navigate through the smoke screen of marketing ploys and false assertions to find what is based on true scientific research. Promotions from commercial programs as well as from the federal government have been known to twist the "evidence" into unreliable recommendations. And most commercial products certainly know how to market improvement programs with seductive styling. In *What Really Matters for Struggling Readers: Designing Research-based Programs* researcher Richard Allington warns, "When we ask about which method, material, or program is most effective, we ask a question that, literally, cannot be answered by referring to the research" (2006, 33).

So how can school leaders with good intentions proceed with confidence in defining quality instruction? Allington proclaims that the answer lies in acknowledging there is no *single* best method to provide quality instruction, but that there are specific instructional *features* proven to make a difference in student achievement. If schools focus on recognizing and building continuity around the proven features or characteristics of evidence-based instruction, they will go a long way toward creating learning organizations where all students win.

The reading workshop and writing workshop frameworks embrace distinctive instructional methods, independent of profit-based agendas. What's more, the instructional features of a workshop approach characteristically emphasize the following proven qualities of instruction:

1. Learning strategies are explicitly modeled (Pearson and Johnson 1978; Pressley et al. 1989; Taylor et al. 2003).

2. Guided practice is differentiated for a range of learners (Pearson et al. 1992; Pearson and Fielding 1991; Swanson and Hoskyn 1998).

3. Lessons are designed to be relevant and meaningful to the learners (Fink 2006; Guthrie et al. 2006).

4. Large blocks of time are reserved for students' continuous reading or writing (Allington and Johnston 2002; Pressley et al. 2001).

5. Periodic assessments and monitoring systems inform instructional decisions (Deno and Marston 2006; Fuchs, Deno, and Mirkin 1984).

6. Descriptive feedback involves students in setting learning goals (Black and Wiliam 1998).

These instructional characteristics may not be obvious to all faculty unless the expected qualities are explicitly stated. Some teachers or administrators might be focused on the mechanisms of implementation (e.g., the mini-lesson, status of the class, or small-group instruction) more than the intended constructs (e.g., promoting strategic thinking and self-monitoring, socially constructing meaning, and designing authentic applications of knowledge). Continuity of the comprehensive literacy vision, however, will be enriched when the norms for evidence-based instruction resonate from a variety of contexts and sources and are reiterated from all angles, such as rubrics of instructional standards, professional development, staff meetings, teacher evaluations, and comments from district leaders, principals, and colleagues.

One action step for communicating instructional expectations would be to collaboratively develop a rating scale or rubric describing quality instruction. Such a tool can be used as a simple reference document to sharpen the instructional focus and to articulate the instructional expectation. The intention of the rating scale would be to define instructional features to practice and to promote. Describing key instructional features in concise and observable terms gives teachers and administrators a common reference point for setting professional goals. It emphasizes instructional characteristics above mechanistic implementation. Figure 7.3 illustrates an example of a rubric for quality instruction based on the evidence-based instructional features expected at Moreland Hills Elementary School.

So one challenge might be to form a representative team of teachers and administrators to identify the evidence-based features of your selected framework and then to collaboratively design a rubric describing each key instructional feature, progressing along a developmental continuum of how it might look and sound. Teachers could use such a rubric as a self-evaluation of lesson design or as a reference to set professional goals in line with the literacy vision. Well-defined quality instruction sets the standard for lesson design based on clear and common qualities, with all students benefiting from quality instruction.

Prioritizing the Core Curriculum: From Inch-Deep Coverage to In-depth Focus

At a recent literacy conference in Ohio, author and researcher Ellin Keene (2006) referred to the enormous volume of state content indicators as a "curriculum obesity" problem. She expressed concern that educators have been distracted from a comprehensible instruction focus because of the vast number of learning indicators weighting every subject area. Educators across the nation are faced with the growing obstacle of massive state content-area learning objectives, or indicators.

Figure 7.3 Rating Scale of Quality Instruction

QUALITY	WHAT IT LOOKS LIKE	RATING
Learning strategies are explicitly demonstrated	Learning targets are clearly stated to students before and during a lesson The lesson focus is on a specific learning strategy Strategies for learning and comprehension are explicitly explained and modeled	1 2 3 4
Guided practice is differentiated among a broad range of learners	All students are invited to practice the skills or strategies demonstrated Methods, materials, and/or pacing are regularly adjusted in response to a range of student needs Tasks and texts are matched to the interests, learning styles, and stages of learners Whole-group, small-group, and individual instruction is routinely provided	1 2 3 4
Lessons are designed to be relevant and meaningful to the learners	New learning is connected to information or experiences familiar to students Lessons are linked to authentic audiences and purposes and motivations Students are invited to co-construct classroom resources with the teacher Choice is built into student activities	1 2 3 4
Large blocks of time are reserved for students' continuous reading or writing	Daily instructional time is efficiently paced to preserve the majority of time for independent reading or writing Students select books that can be read with good accuracy for independent or buddy reading Plenty of interesting reading materials representing a wide range of levels, genres, and styles of writing are easily available to students	1 2 3 4
Periodic assessment and monitoring systems inform instructional decisions	Assessment of reading and writing is used to differentiate grouping and determine learning gaps, interests, and strengths Daily data are gathered in the form of annotated observations or running records Documentation reflects routine monitoring systems Students track progress in some learning areas	1 2 3 4
Descriptive feedback involves students in setting learning goals	Students can explain personal learning goals and what they are expected to know Teacher-to-student conferences name areas of strength and identify manageable areas for improvement Feedback is positive and specific Students are given opportunities to practice constructive feedback with peers	1 2 3 4

SCALE: 1=needs attention; 2=occasionally evident with misconceptions; 3=routinely evident 4= exemplary

Establishing common standards and grade-level objectives across a state is well intentioned. States alleviate the guessing game between district and state expectations and assessments and clearly communicate benchmark learning objectives from preschool through grade twelve. However, the volume of indicators per grade level and subject area causes a scattered and subjective instructional coverage that goes an inch deep and a mile wide or that affects a haphazard system contingent on individual instructional pacing and depth.

The Mid-continent Research for Education and Learning (McREL) calculates, on average, 3,093 benchmarks (or indicators) across various subject areas for preschool through high school. Students spend an estimated 5.6 instructional hours in school each day, about 180 days a year. Education experts Robert Marzano and John Kendall calculate that 9,042 instructional hours are available in thirteen years of schooling. Adequately covering the 3,093 learning indicators, however, would require 15,465 hours, according to conservative McREL calculations. By Marzano and Kendall's estimation, to cover all this content, you would need a twenty-two-year school cycle, from kindergarten through grade twenty-one (Marzano and Kendall 1998).

Education experts (DuFour et al. 2006; Marzano 2007; Reeves 2002; Stiggins et al. 2004) agree that one solution to this curriculum obesity is to focus on a few prioritized grade-level indicators. Accentuating an essential few indicators directs a shared vigilance for academic progress. These become the critical indicators for concentrated instruction and frequent monitoring. The intent is not to restrict the list of indicators covered but instead to recognize that the content load for mastering academic objectives rests more heavily on some indicators than on others. As an extensive list instructional coverage will vary widely; however, a subset of critical indicators creates a common set of priorities for determining which indicators to address in depth and to routinely monitor for progress.

Ideally, when an entire grade level focuses (depth of instruction and assessment) on students' mastery of common, high-priority indicators, we strengthen students' foundation for subsequent learning. Moreover, each teacher can rely on the thorough focused effort of previous instruction.

The Process

A significant action toward aligning instructional continuity at Moreland Hills was prioritizing the academic content indicators within each grade level. When we began this process, the state's standards books were still tightly sealed in cellophane. The challenge was to familiarize ourselves with the new content standards (for each grade and subject area), terminology (e.g., *standard, benchmark, indicators*) and standards categories (e.g., *writing process, writing applications, conventions*), while moving through a process of selecting high-priority indicators.

Although the specific terminology may vary among states or districts, the process of prioritizing grade-level objectives can generically apply. Again, the principle of building momentum with small successes is important to keep in mind.

Within three years, we allocated time for collaborative groups to accomplish the following steps toward sharpening a common focus on the curriculum standards:

1. Prioritize a subset of essential indicators for a grade-level content area
2. Sort the prioritized indicators into grading periods as a pacing guide

Prioritize a Subset of Essential Indicators for a Grade-Level Content Area

Condensing and prioritizing content indicators at Moreland Hills progressed through a cycle with each content area. Grade-level teams worked on consolidating the reading and writing indicators. Then, once the process and intent were clear, two representatives per grade collaborated to identify the essential indicators for math, science, and social studies, resulting in dialogue that integrated a consistent progression of concept development across the grades.

Our first focus was with the writing standards for each grade level. As writing applied across all content areas, we were able to build a common language around the standards and to communicate the intent of the work to all classroom and intervention teachers. Professional release days became our venue for launching the process. For writing and later for reading standards, entire grade-level teams were scheduled one day at a time to meet in our large conference room for a whole day of professional collaboration on one content area. Our primary purpose for the day was to analyze the grade-level standards in writing and agree on eight to twelve objectives of essential learning (DuFour et al. 2006) that should be emphasized, practiced, and monitored for mastery across all classrooms in a grade or subject.

Fortunately, the website for Ohio's department of education posted the content standards organized in two- to three-year progressions of the indicators tied to a common benchmark learning target. After clarifying key terms for categories of information, we highlighted the verbs in each indicator or critical phrases that distinguished responsibility of focus from one grade level to another. For example, students in first grade are expected to *recall* important information about a topic *with teacher assistance*. Students in second grade are expected to *identify* important information about a topic and *write brief notes* about the information. Third graders should be able to identify important information found in *multiple sources* and *sum-*

marize the important findings. The words in italics represent the distinct instructional shift of focus expected from grade to grade. Highlighting these makes the distinctions plain.

Analysis of the distinctions catalyzed conversation about which habits of instruction had to be reined in to meet state expectations and which areas of instruction needed to be enriched. Once the grade-level distinctions were identified and compared, teachers critiqued each indicator, considering three criteria in order to select priorities:

1. Is mastery of this skill/concept necessary for success in subsequent units of study?

2. Is an aspect of this skill/concept unique to this grade level?

3. Is this skill/concept typically difficult for students to master or hard to teach?

The resulting list is not cut and dried. It requires periodic review as populations of students change or as instruction and assessment practices reveal new challenges. But a process of questioning what should be our shared commitment and focus helped us clarify essential curricular objectives. The target is made evident so the aim can be steady and sure. With a list of identified common priorities for curriculum, or essential indicators, each grade-level or subject-area team can plan lessons, critique student work, and monitor student progress, which sharpen our mutual efforts of realizing grander degrees of student success.

Sort the Prioritized Indicators into Grading Periods as a Pacing Guide

Once grade-level indicators for reading and writing have been refined to a focused and manageable subset, it is helpful to organize the pacing of their instruction. A pacing guide becomes a common reference indicating landmarks of learning sequenced monthly or by grading period. New teachers rely on these to plan lesson progressions and to see which instructional focus lies around the bend. Grade-level teams refer to them to maintain an instructional tempo and to design informal checkpoints that monitor student progress.

For this step, we capitalized on various venues. During the summer months, three teachers (two classroom teachers and a reading specialist) used the summer curriculum-writing venue, generating pacing guides in reading, writing, and word study for grade one in two full days of summer work. Tackling one content area at a time, we sorted the essential learnings and common resources onto three three-way charts from September through May (September–November, December–February, and March–May). Each of us envisioned realistic expectations in terms of setting the culture, developing concepts, and transitioning from one instructional focus to the next. This first pacing guide was proposed and refined by that grade level in the fall. Meanwhile, the process and product created during the summer work served as a model for other grade levels to follow as they generated their guides (Figure 7.3).

The common expectation was for each grade to generate pacing guides for reading, writing, and word study. Each grade-level team, however, had a choice of whether to have a month-by-month guide or one that sorted essential learnings by trimester. The value of collaborations among veteran teachers, new teachers, and reading specialists deepened the experience immeasurably. New teachers could identify what they wished had been clearer in their first year. New veteran teachers knew the reality of groundwork and timing necessary to allow for concept development, and reading specialists took advantage of opportunities to intersperse pacing for differentiated instruction as well as for critical monitoring of students performing below benchmarks.

Some grade-level teams opted to use two professional release days and others met in a series of after-school sessions. These pacing guides remain fluid documents, regularly refined in format and content. The process facilitates shared ownership and turns out to be as valuable as the product. The pacing guides become a tool for embedding essential indicators into the daily lesson design in a user-friendly format, used mutually across a grade level and shared with any intervention teachers who work with that grade level.

The targeted indicators promote deliberate time and attention to the mastery of high-priority concepts and skills, while grade-level pacing guides organize those targets for practical instructional plans. The scope and sequence of instruction converge toward a schoolwide focused commitment of improving student learning.

What Can Administrators and School Leaders Do?

INCREASE CONTINUITY. *WHAT RESOURCES AND PRACTICES CAN BE MADE MORE CONSISTENT TO ADVANCE THE GOALS OF YOUR COMPREHENSIVE LITERACY SYSTEM?*

* Communicate the rationale for a prioritized core curriculum.

* Determine an accessible location to house and/or post the essential indicators.

* Once identified, refer to the essential indicators in professional development, collaborative teams, staff meetings, open house, and professional evaluation settings.

DEEPEN PROFESSIONAL LEARNING. *HOW CAN YOU SUPPORT THE COMPREHENSIVE LITERACY GOALS WITH ONGOING PROFESSIONAL DEVELOPMENT?*

* Schedule professional release days per grade level for identifying a concise list of the essential indicators in reading and then again in writing.

* Facilitate vertical dialogue across grade levels regarding prioritized curriculum. Identify gaps as well as commitments for the degree of grade-level mastery.

* Explore instructional implications tied to the essential indicators.

EMPOWER COLLABORATIVE LEADERSHIP. *WHAT OPPORTUNITIES FOR COLLABORATIVE LEADERSHIP WILL EXPAND PARTICIPATION AND ADVANCE THE GOALS OF YOUR COMPREHENSIVE LITERACY SYSTEM?*

* Encourage parents and teachers to share suggestions for ways to communicate the essential indicators to students and families.

* Invite teachers of special areas, such as music and art, to consider ways to enhance students' grasp of essential indicators through the arts.

REALLOCATE RESOURCES. *HOW CAN YOU USE ASSETS YOU ALREADY HAVE IN A WAY THAT WILL ADVANCE THE GOALS OF A COMPREHENSIVE LITERACY SYSTEM?*

* Ask an office secretary or parent volunteer to type the essential indicators into a shared document format.

Making It Your Own: Reflections for a Custom Fit

A. What practices do you want your faculty to know and be able to do?

B. What specific supports will your faculty need in order to customarily implement a prioritized core curriculum?

C. What assets and resources are available to coordinate the supports necessary?		
Space for Professional Development	Time for Professional Development	Expertise
Models to Observe	Professional References	Core Interest Group

D. Think Big, Start Small: Four Simple Steps Forward

1. Challenge each grade level to identify eight to ten reading objectives, tied to the state indicators, to commit to focused instruction.

2. How might those objectives be restated into student-friendly language? (Begining with the phrase "I can...")

3. Facilitate grade levels to compare the state indicators to current units of instruction to find connections and disconnections.

4. Have grade-level groups generate key terminology students will need to know and apply specifically related to state objectives.

Integrating Intervention with Classroom Instruction

If Miriam is a student struggling in reading, we want to provide her with the extra time and expert support necessary to accelerate her reading growth. We want to add to the time she spends reading meaningful continuous text, to stimulate her will to read and learn more, to fortify her capacity to think strategically across the curriculum, and to deepen her understanding of classroom curriculum. To catch up closer to her peers, Miriam will need to achieve at least one and a half years of progress in one year's time. She cannot afford for us to waste her time. It is our moral imperative, as educators, to respond with smart designs for effective, evidence-based instruction and integrated curriculum. To set in motion that rate of accelerated growth, schools need to look at supplementary reading intervention with new eyes.

Supplemental reading intervention refers to models that facilitate extra time and support to struggling readers supplemental to sound classroom reading lessons. A valuable way to organize instructional continuity is through a mutually supporting design integrating supplemental reading intervention with classroom aims. Designing academic support models to coincide with the core classroom instruction increases student success by promoting reciprocity between classroom lessons and supplemental interventions.

Although establishing some common instructional frameworks, such as reading workshop or writing workshop, supports a unified progression for students from grade to grade, connecting intervention with core classroom instruction affects certain students repeatedly. Often, academically at-risk students must make sense of conflicting messages teachers ask them to do to be successful. One remedial reading teacher routinely teaches a long list of words students must know before they read a passage, which implies that they can't read unless they know all the words in the text first. This perpetuates the problem of readers who pronounce words but do not comprehend the text. Then, when these children return to the classroom, the teacher encourages them to problem-solve unknown words or confusing parts using a variety of strategic actions, giving the self-actualizing message that "you can figure out text using the tools you know." In the intermediate grades, students are pulled from science class to attend a small remedial reading group. These struggling readers must then make up the missed assignments and content instruction, which aggravates academic discrepancy. Systems of support often set up the most at-risk learners for extended failure because of mixed messages and fragmented instruction. Instead of closing the achievement gap, some designs for supplementary reading instruction pry the gap wide open.

Remedial intervention can be integrated with core classroom instruction in a number of ways. At Moreland Hills, reading achievement benefits from (1) integrated content, (2) complementary strategies, and (3) flexible tiers of instructional support between classroom instruction and supplementary reading intervention.

Integrated Content

Integrated content means using what is already required classroom curriculum as the core for supplemental support and designing lessons that teach and reinforce strategic thinking around that content. We now work smarter in providing reading intervention by using current study units in math, science, and social studies as catalysts for strategy instruction.

The reading interventionist can use the grade level's science textbook for students to practice studying nonfiction texts, identifying evidence of text structure, or speaking about specific comprehension strategies. Articles, picture books, leveled texts, and short stories tied to a current unit in social studies can be used to preconstruct background knowledge for an upcoming unit on explorers. Providing information up front elevates students to knowledgeable roles in the classroom.

Complementary Strategies

When selecting or designing supplementary interventions, a critical element is how well the strategy instruction in the delivery model complements the strategy instruction in the classroom. Are the instructional precepts similar enough that teachers in different roles will not be giving students contradictory messages about reading or writing tasks? Can the lessons and tools be applied reciprocally between the intervention and the classroom?

Rather than entangling students in opposing messages, we can effectively reinforce strategic behavior when our prompts and expectations line up. For example, at Moreland Hills the Reading Recovery program for first graders directly complements guided reading instruction, like two sides of the same coin. Both emphasize teaching strategic problem-solving behavior over teaching the book, and both build from the point of the reader's knowledge. In addition to Reading Recovery, we've designed supplementary interventions at subsequent grade levels to continue the complementary relationship to classroom strategy instruction. The practice of identifying nonfiction text structures or discussing comprehension strategies reinforces the very language and expectations of the classroom reading instruction. The strategies seen, heard, or used in one setting are seen, heard, and used in another.

Then, professional study and resource development, for classroom teachers and intervention teachers alike, reiterate the kind of instructional prompts, tools, assessments, and responses that further unite teaching and learning across instructional settings. This approach to remedial intervention provides a "planned redundancy" that reinforces experience and understanding along the same concept paths. The best way to get your point across is to repeat it.

Flexible Tiers of Instructional Support

Schools frequently find themselves stretched too thin to accommodate the number of students needing supplemental reading support. The reading specialist's caseload can serve a limited number of small groups for instruction. In addition, research on characteristics of effective reading interventions indicates that student groups of more than three yield ineffective return on academic success (Allington 2004; D'Agostino and Murphy 2004; Swanson and Hoskyn 1998; U.S. Department of Education 2005; Vaughn et al. 2003). An obvious solution is to add more reading teachers so that more small groups can be served, but that thinking is neither cost-effective nor necessary. How to serve students who need extra time and support does not rest in hiring more specialists. Instead, we need to create conditions that multiply dimensions of time and expertise.

Integrated content and complementary strategy instruction are certainly multipliers because they affect students' exposure through redundancy and reciprocity. Schools can further multiply the quantity of students served and accelerated by thinking innovatively about the role of the reading specialist: How can we capitalize on the expertise of reading specialists to extend intensive and expert supplemental reading instruction to all struggling readers?

According to Judge Felix Frankfurter, "It was a wise man who said that there is no greater inequality than the equal treatment of unequals" (1950). At Moreland Hills, reading interventionists design delivery models outside the confines of pullout sessions and rigid student caseloads. We want to maximize our availability to reach a range of learning needs while enhancing the quality of instruction classroom teachers can provide. Our safety net team of academic interventionists implements flexible, tiered instructional support for varying degrees of academic need. The flexibility is created by considering five elements of design for supplementary reading support as illustrated in Figure 7.4.

Figure 7.4 Elements for the Dynamic Delivery of Expert Instruction

DESIGN ELEMENT	EXAMPLES
Kind of instructional support provided by the reading specialist	Briefly introducing instructional techniques to students and their teachers for activating background knowledge, engagement, or vocabulary development embedded within a unit of study
	Consulting with the classroom teachers to plan differentiated instruction, accessible texts, appropriate tasks, or homework adaptations
	Creating customized resource tools for use by the student in the classroom
	Routinely providing in-class, pull-aside tutorial sessions; carrying key manipulatives and materials into the classroom
	Routinely providing pullout intervention sessions
Frequency of sessions	2–5 days a week of additional reading instruction
Length of each intervention session	15–30 minutes of tailored, 1:1 lessons
	20–40 minutes of small-group lessons
Grouping of students for intervention	1:1
	Small groups with common learning targets
	Small groups with complementary skills
Number of weeks devoted to the intervention	Offering varying lengths or alternating intervals for short-term intensive support with a distinct intention to phase out the dependency as soon as possible

Of course, the first line of defense is to minimize the number of struggling readers in the first place by enhancing the quality and quantity of classroom reading instruction. Then, in conjunction with standards of quality classroom instruction, innovative combinations in these intervention design elements constitute differing degrees of support. The dynamic nature of such an array of alternatives opens opportunities to customize intervention for a greater number of students in need.

What Can Administrators and School Leaders Do?

INCREASE CONTINUITY. *WHAT RESOURCES AND PRACTICES CAN BE ALIGNED TO ADVANCE THE GOALS OF YOUR COMPREHENSIVE LITERACY SYSTEM?*

* Identify universal instructional features to encourage in both classroom and intervention instruction.

* Select or critique instructional formats for classroom and intervention design that emphasize complementary features.

* Unify instructional language for consistent prompting, emphasis, and terminology as needed for ease of translation for students, parents, and teachers.

* Unify a common criteria for describing reading behaviors.

DEEPEN PROFESSIONAL LEARNING. *HOW CAN YOU SUPPORT THE COMPREHENSIVE LITERACY GOALS WITH ONGOING PROFESSIONAL DEVELOPMENT?*

* Create opportunities for parents, intervention teachers, and classroom teachers to develop repertories for addressing the needs of struggling learners.

* Provide time and resources for teachers to observe and analyze student performance with targeted focus and professional reflection.

EMPOWER COLLABORATIVE LEADERSHIP. *WHAT OPPORTUNITIES FOR COLLABORATIVE LEADERSHIP WILL EXPAND PARTICIPATION AND ADVANCE THE GOALS OF YOUR COMPREHENSIVE LITERACY SYSTEM?*

* Encourage teams to identify common indicators of academic risk and to develop monitoring systems and checklists to help track progress.

* Encourage intervention teachers and classroom teaches to meet routinely (monthly or each grading period) to review and refine ways to be mutually supportive of struggling students.

REALLOCATE RESOURCES. *HOW CAN YOU USE ASSETS YOU ALREADY HAVE IN A WAY THAT WILL ADVANCE THE GOALS OF YOUR COMPREHENSIVE LITERACY SYSTEM?*

* Design teachers' schedules that provide common planning time for interventionists and classroom teachers. Avoid scheduling duties and other assignments in ways that interfere with this objective.

* Make it a priority to send teams of intervention teachers and classroom teachers to workshops and or conferences that enrich instructional integration.

Making It Your Own: Reflections for a Custom Fit

A. What intervention practices do you want your faculty to know and be able to do?

B. What specific supports will your faculty need in order to customarily integrate classroom and supplementary reading supports?

C. What assets and resources are available to coordinate the supports necessary?		
Space for Professional Development	Time for Professional Developement	Expertise
Models to Observe	Professional References	Core Interest Group

D. Think Big, Start Small: Four Simple Steps Forward

1. Collaboratively compose a common belief statement about readers and writers.

2. Challenge reading intervention teachers to share ways they integrate instruction directly into classroom objectives.

3. Encourage innovative intervention design and delivery.

4. Encourage informal classroom research interviewing struggling readers regarding how they feel about supplemental supports.

Final Word

When teachers control the design of independent realms of instruction, content priorities and principles of quality instruction vary from room to room and student success is left to the chance of either effective or ineffective teaching. However, when district leaders regiment curricular order with mandated programs and materials, only a narrow portion of students benefits from the one-size-fits-all application. Neither extreme is best for kids.

Joining the forces of instructional frameworks, focused curricular attention, instructional pacing, and intervention design into common alignment catapults our potential to affect learning for students and for their teachers, parents, and administrators. We become a community of educators with concurring agendas and resourceful professionalism. We establish a mutually supportive focus, connecting grade levels, content areas, and instructional settings that synchronize concepts, efforts, and intentions. Students experience the choreography of compatible actions as familiar and responsive. Teachers enjoy the balance of continuity and autonomy. We minimize conditions that interfere with learning and maximize habits that integrate learning.

8 — Response-Ability

Developing a Common System of Responding to Literacy Needs

ALTHOUGH IT HAPPENS EACH YEAR, SCHOOLS THAT PROCLAIM
THEIR MISSION IS TO ENSURE LEARNING FOR ALL HAVE NO PLAN OR
STRATEGY FOR RESPONDING TO THE INEVITABLE MOMENT WHEN A
STUDENT IS NOT LEARNING.
—*Richard DuFour et al.*, Whatever It Takes: How Professional Learning
Communities Respond When Kids Don't Learn

Justin is a third grader with great promise. His pockets are weighted with the stuff of fascination: two tarnished keys, a shooter marble resembling an eyeball, three plastic pirates eager for adventure, and a rock. He loves to conjure animated tales of suspense and heroism, but he hates books because kids laugh when they hear him slog through reading aloud. Justin and his mother recently moved from two states away to live closer to his grandma. Now, his new elementary principal is deciding where she will place Justin.

He could be placed in any third-grade class. Each classroom has a relatively even ratio of girls to boys and a similar distribution of diversity and academic performance. The principal determines Justin's placement based on enrollment numbers in each class and assures Justin's mother that no matter where he is assigned, Justin will do just fine. As is common in a lot of schools across the country, the principal makes a quick judgment call and just hopes the placement will be a good match between the teacher's practice and the student's needs. But will a child have the same chance of success no matter where he is placed?

If Justin is placed in Ms. A's class, his needs may be overlooked. Ms. A is in her first year of teaching. She has an inviting demeanor and every moment in her classroom is full of engaging activities and dependable routines. But her inexperience keeps her from recognizing indicators that Justin's learning progress is at risk. She is intently focused on managing the pacing and details of a first year; therefore, quite a bit of time may lapse before she notices Justin's need for additional reading support.

Placement with Mr. B will guarantee that Justin will be tested frequently, but you can be sure no adjustment will be made to accommodate Justin's needs for academic success. Mr. B believes it is the job of the reading specialist, not a classroom teacher, to close the achievement gap between Justin and his peers, and there are never openings for Title I enrollment at this time of year. Justin will be pegged in Mr. B's class as a "low student," and substandard performance will be expected.

If, by chance, Justin is placed in Ms. C's classroom, he will be lucky. She thoughtfully immerses her students in a variety of meaningful literacy activities and informally assesses her students or confers with them on an ongoing basis. Based on her keen observations of notable indicators, she routinely adjusts groupings and designs opportunities for enrichment and practice according to a range of needs. She sets academic goals with her students and helps them achieve those goals.

Unfortunately, *where* Justin is placed *does* matter. His academic fate might even pivot on this casual classroom assignment. It could mean the difference between addressing Justin's reading challenges effectively or compounding his reading issues with weighty layers of frustration and disconnection. In fact, struggling learners fall through the cracks every year largely because of the crevices schools create. We wedge gaps between our independent efforts to monitor student needs, and we allow the criteria for when and how to respond when kids don't learn to be splintered into separate opinions. When a school endorses maverick judgment calls for when and how to respond to learners at risk, its system for monitoring student achievement is left fractured and vulnerable.

You secretly wish you could assign *all* the kids to Ms. C's class. With a universal plan for recognizing and responding to indicators of reading failure, schools can stop playing roulette with improving student success and start guaranteeing timely and effective responses for all students. Parents could rely on the dependability of quality instruction, and principals could assign classroom placement with confidence that each child's progress and needs would be routinely monitored and professionally addressed. By positioning the benchmarks and the expectations for responding into tighter alignment, the cracks in the monitoring system would be minimized.

Pyramid of Academic Response

Why is it that so many educational systems lack specific plans to respond in a timely and systemic way whenever levels of learning drop below the benchmark? You would expect any successful organization with a clear mission to have systems in place that alert teachers when the mission is not met. Richard DuFour, a recognized leader in helping schools develop professional learning communities and meaningful educational reform, uses the following analogy to portray a school's obligation to establish a strategy for responding to learning failure:

You enter a Starbucks shop at 7:00 a.m. secure in the knowledge that Starbucks has a well-defined and well-understood mission—selling overpriced coffee in a comfortable environment. On this particular morning, however, you discover that this Starbucks is out of coffee. Certainly this would strike you as odd since a Starbucks without coffee cannot fulfill its fundamental mission. You would question why the staff had not developed a plan both to monitor the quantity of the coffee in the restaurant and to respond in a timely and systematic way whenever those quantities dropped to a certain level. The absence of a plan would strike you as extremely peculiar and as incongruous with the mission of Starbucks. (DuFour et al. 2004, 41)

Most people would agree that the fundamental mission of a school is to maximize learning for all students; yet teachers don't all monitor the same indicators of risk, and schools seldom have a strategic plan for responding when levels of learning fall below the expected standard.

At Moreland Hills Elementary School, we were frustrated by repeated and inconsistent responses to students' academic needs. An intervention assistance team (IAT) met weekly to help classroom teachers and parents frame goals and then brainstorm interventions to address demanding academic or behavioral issues. It is part of Ohio's requirement for identifying the least restrictive environment to meet students' needs. However, the team's participation from most teachers was discouraging. The same set of classroom teachers would refer three or four students each year and take them through the process of framing goals, identifying and implementing interventions, and collaborating with parents to increase a student's success, whereas other teachers would go for years never referring a single student. Among those who did participate were varying degrees of documentation and student support. Some teachers would come prepared with samples of student work and a list of ways the issue had already been addressed in the classroom; others would arrive at the first meeting ready only to describe their hunches about what was wrong with the child, never having tried a single accommodation.

At a National Educational Services (NES) institute the seed for a unified system of response was planted. There, Richard DuFour challenged his audience to devise a schoolwide plan for quickly identifying the kids who need extra time and support and for automatically providing extra support when it is most needed. DuFour's challenge spurred our safety net team (made of the intervention support teachers) to design and propose the Pyramid of Academic Response (see Figure 8.1)—a sequence of universal actions promoting shared responsibility for student achievement. The proposed pyramid sequence for responding

Figure 8.1 Moreland Hills Elementary School Pyramid of Academic Response

LEVEL 4—ONLY THOSE STUDENTS IDENTIFIED (VIA A MULTIFACTORED ASSESSMENT) AS NEEDING UNIQUE AND SPECIALIZED INTERVENTION:

Generate an individualized education plan with interventions determined by what has worked well for that student during the previous levels of response.

INDICATORS FOR HIGHER LEVEL OF RESPONSE: With interventions routinely in place, student's performance still falls below established benchmark or student's behavior interferes with academic progress of self or peers.

LEVEL 3—A FRACTION OF THE POPULATION OF STUDENTS FROM LEVEL 2 NEED/RECEIVE THESE INTERVENTIONS:

- Classroom teacher refers student to IAT; interventions continue to be documented in class.
- IAT representative works with the teacher to gather documentation, refine the interventions if necessary, and frame 1–3 measurable goals.
- Through IAT, new interventions are selected, implemented, and documented.
- Progress is determined to be either typical or atypical.

INDICATORS FOR HIGHER LEVEL OF RESPONSE: With interventions routinely in place, student's performance still falls below established benchmark or student's behavior interferes with academic progress of self or peers.

LEVEL 2—A SMALLER POPULATION OF STUDENTS NEED/RECEIVE THESE INTERVENTIONS:

- Parents are notified of the specific classroom concerns.
- Classroom teacher administers designated grade-level Classroom Response Assessments.
- Classroom teacher consults with colleague/specialist to generate a Literacy Response Plan of classroom intervention(s) and eligibility for supplemental support is determined.
- Classroom teacher documents classroom accommodations for a designated period of time.

INDICATORS FOR HIGHER LEVEL OF RESPONSE: Student's performance falls below established benchmark or student's behavior interferes with academic progress of self or peers

START HERE

LEVEL 1—ALL STUDENTS RECEIVE THESE INTERVENTIONS:

- Classroom teachers administer the Language Arts Assessments for diagnostic information.
- Students are grouped for reading + word study according to performance and strategy need.
- Classroom instruction differentiates for a range of readers and writers at the level indicated by diagnostic assessments.
- Classroom diagnostic instruction includes systems for noting student responses.

was well received by the rest of our faculty and administrators and reinforced the premise that good first teaching in the classroom is the front line of defense against learning failure.

Beginning at the bottom of the Pyramid of Academic Response, each level represents escalating intensity of focused intervention, ranging from the expertise of general classroom instruction up through an individualized education plan (IEP). Every step of the pyramid intentionally decreases in size to represent the shrinking percentage of students requiring that degree of focused intervention. Together, the levels visually depict the shared ownership of and contribution to academic success for all students.

A Pyramid of Academic Response can be applied to achievement indicators in math, reading, or writing. For simplicity, I will demonstrate how we developed the logistics of a pyramid for responding to indicators of academic breakdown in a student's reading progress.

Level 1 on the pyramid signifies the leading edge of student support: high-quality instruction in every classroom. With cohesive attention to identified elements of quality, teachers and administrators see to it that every classroom meets rigorous standards of instruction and student engagement. A continuity of excellence is expected and inspected. *All* students benefit from this level of proactive daily intervention. There remain certain nonnegotiable criteria expected within the context of individual teacher autonomy and style. These define quality instruction in observable terms and, at Moreland Hills, they include the following:

* Using assessments to inform instruction

* Maintaining routines of monitoring progress and giving feedback to students

* Providing accessible texts for a range of readers

* Demonstrating thoughtful literacy

* Gradually releasing responsibility for independent application to the students

* Designing differentiated instruction for a wide range of learners

* Routinely providing long blocks of uninterrupted time for reading

Michala is a fourth-grade student whose fall literacy assessment reveals she can read and comprehend adequately on benchmark level texts. No real cause for alarm. However, in October, during a routine reading conference, her teacher, Ms. Davis, discovers that Michala selects books for her independent reading based on thickness (the skinnier the better) and compliantly writes in her reading response journal following the model posted on the classroom wall. Michala hasn't yet discovered what kind of books or authors she likes to read.

Michala's teacher recognizes the importance of getting kids hooked on books they love and maintaining the volume of reading necessary for continued progress. Ms. Davis sets a goal with Michala to find out what genre or author causes Michala to lose herself in the book. Ms. Davis describes her own favorite books, gives Michala a reader's inventory for self-reflection, and presents brief book talks on three different texts to help Michala select one based on more than the size, each book connected to a series or similar partner texts.

Michala will prosper because of dependable classroom instruction that includes routine checkpoints with readers, a teacher's knowledge of what matters in engaging learners, caring communication, and involving students in setting and supporting meaningful goals. Student performance that might otherwise slide below a proficient level is continuously monitored and addressed within a typical classroom setting because quality instruction in all classrooms is a well-defined part of the school's culture. Hence, level 1 on the Pyramid of Academic Response is a vital contributor to a whole-school monitoring system.

If a student's performance falls below an expected benchmark despite the quality first teaching, the universal response is to move to level 2: gathering more specific information about the reader and generating an action plan. This level of responsive action is not implemented for every child. It is not usually necessary. Most students thrive in the setting of a sound educational environment. But for those who do not, level 2 requires teachers to take a closer look at what might be obscuring the student's path to success. Level 2 is intended to create a zone of shared responsibility among reading specialists, parents, and classroom teachers before anyone jumps headlong into a series of formal evaluations of student ability and achievement. Action steps for level 2 include the following:

* Administering designated classroom response assessments

* Identifying at-risk reading behaviors on a checklist

* Setting one or two specific goals for reading

* Notifying parents about specific concerns; including parents in setting goals

* Collaboratively generating a literacy response plan of action

* Implementing selected accommodations for a designated span of time

Caleb is a second grader who began the school year reading and writing at adequate levels but seemed to hit a wall as the fall trimester proceeded and the demands for comprehending swelled. Despite efforts by his classroom teacher to coordinate opportunities for Caleb to read to a small group of kindergartners and to provide regular practice with sight word recognition, Caleb's reading level did not progress as hoped. But Caleb was not alone. Caleb's teacher, Miss Moriarty, identified four students in her class who remained below the trimester benchmark at the end of the first grading period.

As part of the school's Pyramid of Academic Response, Miss Moriarty gathered specific information on those four students to glean which specific focus of instruction would accelerate each student's progress. Caleb's teacher had the students write the second-grade "snap words" during word study groups that week. She checked their word recognition on the designated Fry word lists and had each of the four students read and retell a leveled text. She noted fluency performance on a rubric during reading conferences. As Miss Moriarty observed these students in reading groups, conferences, and throughout the assessments, she filled out individual checklists of reading behaviors.

Once the classroom response assessments and the reading behavior checklists were completed, Miss Moriarty met with other second-grade teachers to help identify one or two priorities for every regular education student that was not yet meeting the reading benchmark.

In the process of reviewing documentation, Miss Moriarty realized that Caleb was among two of the four students who needed to build strategies for maintaining meaning across longer stretches of text; however, the other two students needed to become more strategic in word analysis. One group focused on comprehension goals, and the other group concentrate on word-solving strategies. Miss Moriarty then scanned the bank of classroom accommodations, selected techniques for addressing these goals, and set out over the succeeding two months to align her prompting, guided reading lessons, and student conferencing focus to the targeted goals. The students' parents received literacy response plans that specified the teacher's goals and plan of action, and she requested parents' questions and feedback.

In the meantime, the names of all second-grade students identified by their classroom teachers as performing below the benchmark were forwarded to the reading specialists, and plans for supplemental intervention were coordinated as needed. For some students, this meant simply that the specialist would generate resources to make classroom implementation clear and manageable. In other cases, the intervention teacher co-planned in-class routines or provided short-term services outside of the classroom integrated with the literacy response plan goals.

Level 2 of the Pyramid of Academic Response facilitated a united response across all classrooms to delve more deeply and collect enough information to target specific goals while unvaryingly communicating to specialists which students needed additional expertise to spark accelerated growth. Actively integrating efforts among students, classroom teachers, parents, and reading specialists is a significant feature of level 2.

Because of the cooperative monitoring and responding set in motion within levels 1 and 2, only a fraction of the students involved at level 2 must proceed to an even higher degree of focused intervention on the pyramid. Level 3 of the pyramid primarily involves the process of the IAT. Components in this process vary from state to state and from school to school. At one time, our response was to jump from classroom support (level 1) to the IAT process (level 3), wherein the child would undergo formal testing to be identified for special education services. Now, with the literacy response plan embedded within our universal Pyramid of Academic Response, many students reach a successful command of the concepts and strategies necessary to accelerate progress and reach their benchmarks without formal intervention.

Level 3 of the pyramid incorporates the valuable information gained from implementing the literacy response plan. The six to eight weeks of literacy response plan accommodations are not discarded for a new flavor-of-the-month intervention when a student is referred to the intervention team. Classroom teachers come to the initial intervention team meeting of parents and educational support specialists and are prepared to describe a student's performance and any proven accommodations. That practical feedback can streamline the team's next steps. The team does not have to begin at square one because a period of classroom intervention has already been provided.

In the middle of his third-grade year, Noah's academic progress depended on more than classroom and supplemental reading support. His classroom teacher had coordinated learning targets for Noah's literacy response plan with his reading intervention teacher but Noah's instructional level of reading remained on a plateau for months. Noah's case was referred to and scheduled for the IAT. Since Noah's teachers concentrated on mutual goals and regularly implemented accommodations in the preceding months, documentation revealed the degree of intense support required for Noah to maintain his level of achievement.

His teachers' documentation of progress and presentation of work samples made it possible to cut the IAT process directly to setting new goals and supplementing support with short-term specialized services, while the school psychologist administered evaluations of Noah's receptive language and cognitive processing. Before the literacy response plan, this process was bogged down whenever a teacher arrived with no clear data, no analysis of what might be contributing to the deficiency, and no evidence of providing specific accommodations.

The highest level on the Pyramid of Academic Response is reserved for the rare occasion when a student's reading progress can be successful only through intensive and extraordinary modifications to the curriculum or educational setting. Level 4 is directly aligned with the legal conditions each state defines for identifying students for special education.

Noah and Halley were both referred to the IAT process (level 3 on the pyramid) by teachers who had implemented literacy response plans and who were still not seeing expected progress. For Noah, the speech and language evaluation and the short-term sessions with the speech pathologist revealed a slight deficit in receptive language. New accommodations for visual cues and breaking directions into smaller chunks of information proved successful in improving Noah's reading. His teacher's journey up the Pyramid of Academic Response stopped at level 3.

Halley's IAT process took her teacher on a different track. Halley's evaluation confirmed a considerable discrepancy between her high cognitive ability and her challenges in reading. Halley was articulate and creative, yet reading stumped her. To stimulate successful progress, it was determined that Halley needed special education services. An individual education plan (level 4 on the pyramid) described the specialized goals and services to set in place for Halley's academic growth.

Preparing for Level Two of the Pyramid: The Literacy Response Plan

Can an effective and timely response be guaranteed from classroom to classroom regardless of Justin's teacher assignment? To answer with a confident "yes," four critical elements need to be in place and applied across the school:

1. A plan to monitor the quality of instruction in your school (see Chapter 7)

2. Benchmark levels set for established checkpoints throughout the year (see Chapter 5)

3. Observable indicators describing academic progress that is "at risk"

4. A strategic plan to respond to indicators of at-risk performance in a timely and systematic way.

The literacy response plan names the observable indicators all teachers will watch for and delineates the strategic plan for responding to students who demonstrate risk factors in reading progress.

Rolling Out a Literacy Response Plan

Zooming in on level 2, a literacy response plan is made up of the following feature resources (in order of application):

1. *Classroom Response Assessments.* These are the designated assessments to be administered

by the classroom teacher within a specific time frame to students whose performance falls below the expected benchmark. Since we have established the benchmark reading levels corresponding to each grading period, the classroom response assessments (see Figure 8.2) are given at the beginning of each grading period to the students who did not reach the benchmark.

Figure 8.2 Moreland Hills School (MHS) Classroom Response Assessments for Literacy

GRADE	SEPTEMBER FOR ALL STUDENTS (OCTOBER FOR KINDERGARTEN)	REQUIRED FOR ALL STUDENTS PERFORMING BELOW THE READING BENCHMARK AT THE END OF GRADING PERIOD ADMINISTER IN DECEMBER FOR GRADES 1–5 ADMINISTER IN JANUARY FOR KINDERGARTEN	MAY FOR ALL STUDENTS
K	Kindergarten State Diagnostic Test and MHS Language Arts Assessment System	ABC Checklist Concepts of Print Picture-Assessment of Initial Sound Knowledge	MHS Language Arts Assessment System
1	MHS Language Arts Assessment System	Snap Words Checklist (Sept/Nov) Form A, DRA Fry Word Recognition: Lists 2, 3, 4	MHS Language Arts Assessment System Grade-Level Writing Prompt
2	MHS Language Arts Assessment System	Form A, DRA Fry Word Recognition: Lists 3, 4, 5	MHS Language Arts Assessment System Grade-Level Writing Prompt
3	MHS Language Arts Assessment System	Form A, DRA, or Record of Oral Reading on Landmark Text	MHS Language Arts Assessment System Grade-Level Writing Prompt
4	MHS Language Arts Assessment System	Form A, DRA, or Record of Oral Reading on Landmark Text	MHS Language Arts Assessment System
5	MHS Language Arts Assessment System	Form A, QRI, or Record of Oral Reading on Landmark Test	MHS Language Arts Assessment System Grade-Level Writing Prompt

2. *Checklist of At-Risk Indicators for Reading.* Once assessments have been given and scored, the next step is for the classroom teacher to complete a checklist of at-risk indicators for reading (see Figure 8.3) for every student whose reading performance falls below benchmark. In Figure 8.3, four strategies are boxed together at the top of the column

entitled Early Skills/Strategies. These four strategies refer to reading behaviors Marie Clay (1993) stresses as a top priority for kids to get under control while they begin to learn how to read and attend to print. The teacher works alone or with other colleagues to check any characteristic reading behaviors listed on this checklist based on analysis of the assessment information and anecdotal observations during reading instruction. Looking over the checklist, classroom teachers select one or two priority goals to target with focused accommodations for six to eight weeks.

Figure 8.3 Checklist of At-Risk Indicators for Reading

Adapted from Moreland Hills Elementary School Teachers' Literacy Response Plan, 2004/2005 and Euclid Reading Specialists, 2006.

EMERGENT SKILLS/STRATEGIES	EARLY SKILLS/STRATEGIES	DEVELOPING SKILLS/STRATEGIES

☐ Lacks verbal phonological awareness:
  * Rhyming
  * Blending Sounds
  * Isolating Sounds
☐ Lacks flexible/instant letter recognition
☐ Lacks flexible/instant letter formation
☐ Does not understand that letters represent sounds
☐ Lacks background knowledge and expressive vocabulary for common objects, animals, story language, and concepts
☐ Does not locate known words in flexible contexts/fonts
☐ Confuses or is unfamiliar with print terminology such as *word / letter / capital / lowercase / period / question mark*
☐ Confuses left-to-right directionality on the word or text level
☐ Does not demonstrate crisp 1:1 pointing/matching
☐ Does not recall information from stories read aloud
	LACKS EARLY READING STATEGIES:
	☐ Does not demonstrate routine left-to-right directionality
	☐ Does not routinely demonstrate a crisp 1:1 match, pointing to each word
	☐ Does not locate words based on the first sound
	☐ Does not locate or monitor for known sight words embedded in text
	
	☐ Does not stop and monitor when meaning breaks down
	☐ Does not stop and monitor at a gross visual mismatch (known words or initial letter)
	☐ Does not stop and monitor when sentence structure doesn't sound right
	☐ Frequently appeals for help; gives up easily
	☐ Lacks phrasing and fluency
	☐ Retains limited recognition of appropriate sight words
	☐ Misreads punctuation, affecting comprehension
	☐ Does not apply flexible decoding strategies
	☐ Shows many misconceptions regarding literal information
	☐ Does not sequence events or details
	☐ Does not make predictions for plausible outcomes
		☐ Avoids/resists reading
		☐ Does not have a strategy for systematically decoding polysyllabic words
		☐ Does not reread to deepen understanding
		☐ Does not efficiently scan text for key information (to answer questions and/or to locate supportive evidence)
		☐ Does not use nonfiction text features to gather information before and during reading
		☐ Does not recognize specific nonfiction text structures
		☐ Does not discern important information from interesting details
		☐ Does not easily identify main idea
		☐ Does not identify details that support a main idea
		☐ Does not gather and sustain information across longer texts
		☐ Does not comprehend vocabulary or terminology basic to text/plot/meaning
		☐ Does not effectively summarize the gist of the text
		☐ Does not infer meaning (theme, humor, generalizations, time shifts, characterizations, symbolism...)

3. *"If…Then…" Bank of Classroom Accommodations.* Every phrase listed on the checklist of at-risk indicators for reading directly corresponds to a brainstormed collection of proven classroom accommodations. These make up the bank of classroom accommodations. Figure 8.4 shows just one sample at-risk behavior for each of the three reading levels and their corresponding accommodations. A blank "If…Then…" form for you to use is provided in Appendix E. Appendix F gives a complete list of the at-risk reading behaviors identified by Moreland Hills teachers, with corresponding banks of classroom accommodations. There is a detailed bank of accommodations for those behaviors considered to be risk-indicators for students just emerging into reading, for early readers still navigating the early strategies and cuing systems, and for developing readers who may face more sophisticated challenges. Teachers select one or two accommodations fitting each of the goals set, keeping in mind a good match for the student and manageability for routine application.

4. *The Literacy Response Plan Form.* This form is simply the documentation of the goals and accommodations selected. The literacy response plan form (Figure 8.5 and Appendix G) serves as a record of the commitment made for the succeeding six to eight weeks and a reminder of which accommodations will be implemented. The classroom teacher may opt to complete a form for individual students or for a group of students who would benefit from the same goals and accommodations in his or her classroom.

Figure 8.4 Sample At-Risk Reading Behaviors and Corresponding Sample Classroom Accommodations

EMERGENT	
IF A STUDENT…	**THEN…**
Lacks verbal phonological awareness: * Rhyming * Blending Sounds * Isolating Sounds	Expose to nursery rhymes and other poems and chants with much rhythm and rhyme
	Provide opportunities for repeated listening to songs, poems, and chants
	Practice choral "reading" of familiar song lyrics, poems, chants, refrains
	Play "Guess My Word," segmenting sounds of a single-syllable word
	Use Elkonin sound boxes, pushing tokens for each sound in single-syllable words
	Clap the rhythm of first and last names to hear syllables
	Play "I spy something that rhymes with…"
	Use picture cards or sets of items for initial and final sound isolation

EARLY	
IF A STUDENT...	THEN...
Does not demonstrate routine left-to-right directionality	Explicitly model 1:1 pointing while reading aloud, thinking aloud for return sweep, left page before right page, and looking left to right across new words
	Ask student to point to where the reader should start to read
	Use big books or enlarged poems to demonstrate left-to-right reading
	Arrange magnetic letters in ABC order and have the student use a pointer to name the letters
	Arrange magnetic letters in ABC order, varying the lines of print in vertical groupings: ABCD EFG...
	Create a board game where the pawns move along a path from left to right, top to bottom
	Have the student "read" the alphabet chart, with a pointer, moving from left to right
	Have student drop and count pennies into egg cartons or other grid-molded containers, left to right

DEVELOPING	
IF A STUDENT...	THEN...
Avoids or resists reading	Seek student's interests; give an interest inventory
	Help student with ways to self-select books ("just right," read blurb on back, author's notes, first few paragraphs)
	Celebrate successes; comment explicitly about the strategies observed
	Lighten the workload (shorter texts, shared reading with a buddy, fewer extensions or questions)
	Set the student up for success; teach the student what he/she needs to know to be successful
	Set a goal with the student
	Try mysteries, humor, nonfiction, or author series to pique interest
	Instruct at independent level for a period of time to build confidence
	Conference more frequently and check on reading accuracy/fluency/comprehension
	Graph the number of books/pages/passages read each week/month
	Spend more time talking informally about books (book talks or book recommendations)
	Respond more frequently to student journal entries about books/reading

Figure 8.5

LITERACY RESPONSE PLAN FOR SMALL GROUPS

Group of Students: _____ Classroom Teacher: _____ Date of Plan: _____

Specialist(s) Consulted: _____ Date(s): _____

A. Targeted Goal: _____

Intervention Commitment: (Select from "If…Then" menu)

(1)_____

(2)_____

Date:	Date:	Date:	Comments/Observations:
____	____	____	
____	____	____	
____	____	____	
____	____	____	

B. Targeted Goal: _____

Intervention Commitment: (Select from "If…Then" menu)

(1)_____

(2)_____

Date:	Date:	Date:	Comments/Observations:
____	____	____	
____	____	____	
____	____	____	
____	____	____	

A Process for Developing Your Own Literacy Response Plan Resources

To facilitate a process for collaboratively developing a literacy response plan, the trek moved along in a different sequence. We created the following (in order of resource development):

1. "If…Then…" Bank of Classroom Accommodations

2. Checklist of At-Risk Indicators for Reading

3. Classroom Response Assessments

4. The Literacy Response Plan Form

Gathering groups of classroom teachers and reading specialists, we started the process of developing a universal literacy response plan by listing some of the observable behaviors often witnessed when a student's reading is not progressing smoothly and by generating ways to address each of those categories of reading challenge. From there, we determined what straightforward but reliable assessments would give classroom teachers more detailed information or specifically characterize a student's reading strengths and challenges. The last resource to be developed was the form for documenting goals and accommodations—the literacy response plan of action.

Generating a Bank of Classroom Accommodations

The most practical resource to come out of the literacy response plan was the bank of classroom accommodations. Its primary value is that the collection of classroom interventions was generated *for* classroom use *by* the classroom teachers and merges knowledge, experienced observations, and applications tested by classroom teachers, reading specialists, and renowned experts. By enticing teachers away from their isolated kingdoms, we unearthed a treasure trove of collective intelligence.

Of course, for you the easy way would be to photocopy the bank of classroom accommodations developed by the Moreland Hills kindergarten through grade five teachers. That would lead your staff two steps forward and three steps backward. The value of the process of developing a bank of accommodations is priceless and would be lost if the focus was on distributing the products of the literacy response plan (i.e., the bank of accommodations, the checklist of at-risk reading behaviors, and the action plan form).

As a literacy leader, your time is precious, and you don't want to waste time (for you or for the teachers) reinventing the wheel; yet, you recognize the advantage of group process in expanding ownership and revealing understandings. Let me suggest a viable solution that can be efficient and will evoke meaningful professional dialogue: Use the general framework and some of the interventions from Moreland Hills' bank of accommodations to spur ideas from your staff.

Here's how we set up opportunities for teachers at Moreland Hills to create our own bank of accommodations. These recommendations can work for your teachers, too:

1. *Provide a block of uninterrupted time for each grade-level team.* First, a half-day release session was scheduled for each grade from kindergarten through grade five; one grade-level team met in the morning for three hours and a different grade-level team met after lunch for three hours. Substitute teachers who released grade four teachers moved to the fifth-grade rooms in the afternoon. By meeting in grade-level groupings, teachers benefited from the commonality of experiences regarding the unique challenges readers of specific grade levels face. Sometimes the disadvantage of vertical groupings can be too much diversity in practical application, and a tendency to address issues in a generalized manner diminishes personal connection.

2. *Facilitate a process for listing commonly problematic reading behaviors and generating a bank of class-room accommodations addressing each problem.* Before each three-hour session with a grade-level team, I set up a fresh new grid of the "If…Then…" chart (see Figure 8.4) on a wide dry erase board. Professional texts with easy reference to evidence-based interventions were distributed around the table. I opened each session by stating the purpose: to name reading behaviors that signal cause for concern and what teachers can do in the classroom to attend to those behaviors. Then I invited teachers to use the resources on the table as well as their own rich experiences of observing and responding to readers.

"We're going to begin by listing out the kinds of reading challenges you see on a regular basis in your classrooms." I stand with marker ready to record their suggestions. "What do you notice readers struggling with? How might you complete the sentence: If a student…" I let my unfinished statement prompt teachers to share reading behaviors often observed in their own classrooms.

Lynne follows my lead and calls out one classic reading issue, "…doesn't comprehend what he reads." Lynne is a diagnostician when it comes to her struggling readers. She scrutinizes the needs of every reader in her class and today she begins the listing.

"Thank you. Would you elaborate on that? What are some indications that a reader is not comprehending?" I prompt. For the tool to be useful for monitoring and addressing reading progress, it needs to explicitly represent observable reading behaviors that typically raise a red flag.

"He can't summarize the story," replies Lynne, "or else he can't tell what information is important to the topic from what is not."

"OK. So if a student *doesn't summarize the gist of a passage*, that would be one indication of concern." I record that phrase in the first block under "*If a Student….*" "Or if she *doesn't discern important information from interesting details*, that would be another indication that comprehension is breaking down." I record this paraphrase in the next box down on the chart. "What else would indicate a red flag to you?"

"To piggyback on what Lynne said, a student might have trouble comprehending if he doesn't understand the key vocabulary," Diane adds. "Maybe he isn't using context clues or maybe he just never heard of a word, like in the case of an ELL [English language learner] student."

The conversation and recording of ideas continue until we've compiled an exhaustive list of reading problems encountered in classrooms. Along the way, we became aware of mutual indicators to watch for as we monitor readers.

Once reading challenges are listed, we shift our attention to the right-hand side of the *If…Then* chart. Next to each challenge, we list several classroom accommodations teachers have used.

"All right, now we're going to brainstorm possible interventions you could provide within a regular classroom setting. Think about what would be both effective and reasonable to implement while you're managing a whole class of students on a daily basis," I explain as I snap the top on the red marker and pick up a blue one. "Let's start with the first one. What is it about the task of summarizing that can be hard for readers? Which instructional techniques are suggested in these resources or have you found in your experience to successfully help students learn to summarize?" Classroom teachers and reading specialists alike define what skills are required of a reader to summarize a text. They scan texts for evidence-based recommendations and contribute practical suggestions. As the bank of classroom accommodations fills out, we expose the simple genius of shared knowledge.

3. *Watch for opportunities to affirm examples of evidence-based practice and to clarify misconceptions.* The discourse that ensued from every grade-level grouping was remarkably eye-opening for me. It gave voice to expert suggestions from peers, fortifying commendable interventions with classroom credibility. It also provided authentic purpose for professionals to reread the recommendations of mentor educators and restock our repertoire of instructional tools. In addition, the conversation revealed some notable misconceptions, raising opportunities for "teachable moments" when teachers asked, "Isn't reading fluency the same as speed reading?" "Are we supposed to teach nonfiction?" "What does a reader need to know and do in order to identify the main idea, and how can you help readers to do that?"

4. *Synthesize the ideas into one resource template.* Once all grade-level groups had a chance to generate ideas, our safety net team of reading interventionists collected the *If…Then…*charts of reading challenges and correlating classroom interventions to consolidate the information into a common resource of ideas. The literacy team or a volunteer group of teachers and literacy leaders could perform this step. It is unnecessary to involve the entire faculty at this point in the process.

Our safety net team synthesized the collection of reading challenges and accommodations to make a valuable and easily accessible document. We expected some overlap, of course, because striving readers are confronted with similar difficulties across a range of grade levels. But wherever there was duplication of identified challenges or interventions, we consolidated the information. Also, as we sorted the suggestions, we were mindful that some accommodations were better suited for intermediate readers, while others matched best with primary levels. We divided the reading behaviors into three general categories of reading development.

a. *Emergent*: aspects of reading readiness such as rhyming, sound segmentation, sound blending, letter-sound associations, concepts of print, and recall of general story.

b. *Early*: aspects of early strategies and skills such as one-to-one matching, attention to initial sound, monitoring a meaning and visual match, self-correcting, fluency, flexible decoding, sequential retelling of story elements.

c. *Developing*: aspects of developing sophistication in reading such as having reading interests, inferring vocabulary and meaning from context, gathering and sustaining information across long stretches of text, setting a reading purpose, and recognizing text structures.

This organization gave the resource a user-friendly layout for teachers to identify highest leverage priorities. In cases where a student's foundational knowledge of an earlier stage remains challenged, developmental gaps are made more visible by the three-column progression of the checklist of at-risk reading behaviors.

The process deepened mutual understanding of the need for a timely and universal response plan. Conversations among classroom teachers and reading interventionists revealed the significance of our mismatched expectations. Because of the joint effort, we generated a practical resource of proven classroom interventions and invigorated a fresh look at age-old dilemmas on how to revive readers.

Creating a Checklist of At-Risk Indicators

Within the literacy response plan, the checklist of at-risk indicators is the simplest resource to produce. The phrases contained on this three-column list (see Figure 8.3) transfer directly from the reading challenges teachers listed under *"If a student…"* on the bank of classroom accommodations organizer. In an intentional replication, teachers can link a direct connection between a reading behavior (on the checklist) and a possible accommodation for that behavior (on the bank of classroom accommodations). The three columns represent a developmental progression of the foundational knowledge and strategies needed for success and engagement in reading.

Selecting the Classroom Response Assessments

If your school is like most, you suffer from what Robert Waterman (1987) refers to as the DRIP syndrome: data rich but information poor. You have more than enough statistics and data to shuffle through for decades, but not enough information to design focused instructional goals. What transforms data into usable information is precise feedback. Teachers need feedback on exactly which strategies a student uses or neglects, and students need descriptive details about what they can do to improve reading.

To select the common set of assessments to be administered when student performance is below the benchmark expectation, the information gathered must translate directly into lesson applications in the classroom.

Three criteria stand out. The classroom response assessments need to be practical, manageable, and timely.

1. *Practical.* The assessment can specifically inform instructional plans with practical information about a student's strengths and areas for improvement. It might include particular information such as what aspect of fluency is most challenging, which words are instantly recognized, to what degree the student is monitoring for meaning, what level of word decoding is applied at difficulty, and whether the reader is more challenged by literal or inferential comprehension. It needs to provide practical information teachers can use immediately.

2. *Manageable.* If the assessments themselves are too cumbersome to administer, they will take teachers and students away from valuable instruction. And if they require extensive item analysis, teachers will balk at the burden. Let's face it. Classroom response assessments have to be quick to endure the reality test of classroom logistics.

3. *Timely.* Classroom response assessments need to be given immediately when students' achievement is identified as "below benchmark." The timetable should present at least two assessment rounds in a given year, allow a reasonable time to implement selected accommodations, and stick to a limited window of time for completion.

The whole idea of common classroom response assessments is to create a school culture of responding immediately and professionally to students in need. Together, we can narrow the achievement gap. By regularly monitoring progress and routinely gathering more specific information on the struggling readers, academic progress can be accelerated with timely interventions tailored to particular needs.

The "Basic Response" versus a Failure to Launch

Fall always brings an onslaught of busy-ness with room setup, individualized assessments, preparation for curriculum night, and the swirl of requests from parents, administrators, and students. In our first year of implementing the literacy response plan, we didn't consider that. We thought it would be realistic to expect documentation on the response plan for each student who started the year below the expected reading level. Wrong! That small addition of paperwork and analysis just about stopped the system of response in its tracks. I expected to see smoldering tire treads on the hallway floors. There is always a delicate balance between what is manageable and what students need to accelerate progress.

We learned from our initial "failure to launch" and put a more manageable and effective common response system in place: the basic literacy response (see Figure 8.6). The basic literacy response is a general plan for instructional focus rather than an individualized plan, yet the areas of focus are unique to each grade level. We identified recurrent patterns of concept or strategy challenges for struggling readers entering each grade. We considered the question, "In addition to the strategy instruction and practice built into the fall culture-building lessons, what few areas of focus need to be brought to mastery early in the school year for reading success?"

Figure 8.6 Basic Literacy Response
Recommendations by grade level of foundational reading instruction for students performing below the benchmark as the year begins

K	1	2	3	4	5
Letter identification Rhyming Oral sound blending	Early Strategies: 1:1 Matching Sound-symbol associations for consonants Applying the first sound along with meaning as cues for word predictions Recognizing core words embedded in text	Building instant sight word recognition Building familiarity with common short-vowel rimes and how one known word can extend to many new words Fix-up strategies: *Self-monitoring errors (stopping and noticing errors) *Initiating problem-solving (Reread, What would make sense here? What do I already know about this word?) Reading with phasing and fluency	Extending instant sight word recognition Building familiarity with common long-vowel clusters Fix-up strategies: *Self-monitoring errors (stopping and noticing errors) *Initiating problem-solving with a variety of strategic actions Reading with phasing and fluency	Initiating interest in reading Fix-up strategies: *Self-monitoring errors (stopping and noticing errors) *Initiating problem-solving with a variety of strategic actions Periodically summarizing the gist across increasingly long portions of text Reading with phasing and fluency	Initiating interest in reading Setting a purpose for reading Recognizing text structures and text features Reading with phasing and fluency

I hesitate to make the recommendations tied to the basic literacy response. I never want to suggest a canned solution to the varied complexities raised by readers. But rather than postponing action while assessments are given and analyzed and while guided reading observations are collected, the basic plan names the area of focus most necessary to give struggling readers a strong foundation. To focus immediate instructional accommodations without delay, the basic literacy response recommends specific areas in which teachers and students need to focus attention and practice as the school year begins.

A Mutual Time Frame for Responding

Our elementary school runs on a trimester time frame. The first trimester extends from the end of August through the first week in November. The second trimester spans from the second week of November through the last week in February. The final trimester stretches from March through June. Figure 8.7 illustrates the sequence of responding to students performing below the reading benchmarks.

Once a universal response plan is set into motion, here's how Justin's scenario would change:

Justin is new to your school and could be placed into any third-grade class. The principal determines Justin's placement based on enrollment numbers in each class and confidently assures Justin's mother that no matter where he is assigned, Justin will do just fine.

If Justin is placed in Ms. A's class, his needs will be carefully monitored. Ms. A is in her first year of teaching, and she has resources to help her recognize and respond to Justin's reading difficulty in a timely and professional fashion. Despite feeling overwhelmed with managing the pacing and juggling the details of a first year, Ms. A refers to the basic response plan to design explicit instruction for Justin and opportunities for his practice. Routine reading conferences help Ms. A to recognize which students in her class still fall below the established benchmark at the end of the first grading period. Without delay, she administers the classroom response assessments and fills out the checklists of observed behaviors. Then she meets with colleagues to set specific goals for Justin's reading success. By December, a tailored literacy response plan of accommodations matched to Justin's needs is launched.

Placement with Mr. B will guarantee that Justin's reading performance will be monitored frequently. Because of schoolwide expectations, adjustments will also be made to accommodate what Justin needs for academic success. Even if Title I caseloads are full, when Mr. B writes his literacy response plan, he will consult with the reading specialist to learn new ways to help close the achievement gap between Justin and his peers. Mr. B will be pleasantly surprised at Justin's growth and discover that Justin can meet the next benchmark without being pulled out of class for a supplemental reading class.

Figure 8.7 One-Year Time Tables for Responding

TIME OF YEAR	EXPECTED TEACHER RESPONSE	FEATURE RESOURCES
All year	Monitor student progress with reading conferences and records of oral reading	Record of oral reading Reading conference form
First four weeks of school (August/September)	Administer and interpret common grade-level assessments to set instructional goals	Language Arts Assessment System Benchmark Reading Levels
First trimester (August through beginning of November)	Provide extra time and focused instruction targeting areas recommended on the basic literacy response for students who perform below the fall benchmark	Basic literacy response chart
End of October	Identify students performing below the benchmark in reading	Record of oral reading Observations from reading instruction
November	Administer the designated classroom response assessments to students performing below benchmark Fill out checklist of reading behaviors	Classroom response assessments Checklist of at-risk reading indicators
December	Work in teams to write literacy response plans for students falling below benchmark; begin implementing the targeted accommodations	Literacy response plan form
December through February	Routinely implement targeted accommodations; confer weekly about specific goal(s) with students at risk	Record of oral reading Reading conference form
End of second trimester	Measure progress on goals and reading levels of students on a literacy response plan; invite parents and colleagues to set new goals or accommodations if a student remains below the benchmark level for reading	Literacy response plan form
March through May	Routinely implement targeted accommodations; confer weekly about specific goal(s) with students at risk	Record of oral reading Reading conference form
May	Administer common grade-level assessments to determine end-of-year performance	Language Arts Assessment System Benchmark reading levels

No matter where he is placed, Justin will benefit from a classroom that offers timely and effective classroom intervention. Differences in teaching styles and environments can be celebrated in the context of deliberate continuity in responding. Structuring the literacy response plan within a universal Pyramid of Academic Response frames the expectation: *how* a teacher responds to readers remains a discretionary choice; *when* and *whether* a teacher responds is no longer optional.

What Can Administrators and School Leaders Do?

INCREASE CONTINUITY. *WHAT RESOURCES AND PRACTICES CAN BE MADE MORE CONSISTENT TO ADVANCE THE GOALS OF YOUR COMPREHENSIVE LITERACY SYSTEM?*

* Establish and communicate a time frame for timely and targeted responses.

* Post and refer to the Pyramid of Academic Response.

* Reiterate deadlines for documentation and reporting which students perform below established benchmarks.

DEEPEN PROFESSIONAL LEARNING. *HOW CAN WE SUPPORT THE COMPREHENSIVE LITERACY GOALS WITH ONGO-ING PROFESSIONAL DEVELOPMENT?*

* Provide study and practice for identifying age-appropriate learning targets.

* Organize routines for observing and critiquing student work samples and for teachers to target one or two learning goals based on observations.

* Study instructional techniques proven to positively impact student achievement.

EMPOWER COLLABORATIVE LEADERSHIP. *WHAT OPPORTUNITIES FOR COLLABORATIVE LEADERSHIP WILL EXPAND PARTICIPATION AND ADVANCE THE GOALS OF YOUR COMPREHENSIVE LITERACY SYSTEM?*

* Facilitate the process for teachers to generate "if...then" charts listing classroom accommodations linked to typical deficit reading behaviors.

* Encourage collaborative teams of educators and parents to create or organize ready resources as accommodative tools, centers, or focus lessons that support struggling readers.

REALLOCATE RESOURCES. *HOW CAN YOU USE ASSETS YOU ALREADY HAVE IN A WAY THAT WILL ADVANCE THE GOALS OF A COMPREHENSIVE LITERACY SYSTEM?*

* Schedule a week when teachers are expected to work with colleagues to complete literacy response plans for low-performing learners; provide substitute teachers as needed.

Making It Your Own: Reflections for a Custom Fit

A. What academic response practices do you want your faculty to know and be able to do?

B. What specific supports will your faculty need in order to customarily implement timely and targeted practices of responding to indicators of academic risk?

C. What assets and resources are available to coordinate the supports necessary?		
Space for Professional Development	Time for Professional Development	Expertise
Models to Observe	Professional References	Core Interest Group

D. Think Big, Start Small: Four Simple Steps Forward

1. Begin a routine expectation for teachers to report names of students performing below the grade-level expectation in reading at the end of each grading period to the principal.

2. Facilitate a process for teachers to generate "if…then" charts listing classroom accommodations linked to typical deficit reading behaviors.

3. Invite collaborative teams to analyze work samples of one low-performing reader together and consider what instructional actions might advance the student's learning.

4. Motivate informal classroom research to examine possibilities for increasing time students spend reading throughout the school day.

9 — ...and Miles to Go...

EXCELLENCE IS NOT AN ACT. IT IS A HABIT.
—Aristotle

I f you are a homeowner, you know the reality of continuous improvement plans. My husband, Paul, and I have renovated five houses on tight budgets. We always seem to buy the ones listed as "a handyman's dream," with plenty of projects to keep us busy for years. Before any part of the renovation work commences, we take a full inventory of where the assets lie and what will (eventually) need to be changed. We take into account the structural and aesthetic affects we want to achieve to determine which walls will remain and which ones will need to be torn down. Although every wall is badly in need of paint or wallpaper from the start, we know it would be a waste of time and materials to work on a wall that will eventually be changed or eliminated. Budget constraints along with the implications of living amid the mess of construction play into the decisions of which projects we initiate and to what degree. On top of the plans for major renovations, the list of improvements and repairs that typically accompanies home maintenance continues to grow faster than the work can get completed. It's a wonder anyone chooses to own a house.

The process of developing a comprehensive literacy system has been a major renovation of continuous improvement. The teachers and administrators at Moreland Hills Elementary School have proudly put a great many structures in place that align intentions and create a mechanized system to support students' academic success. The monthly literacy team has become a source for continuous feedback and action, sustaining supports for classroom implementation and grade-level continuity.

Our building budget reflects some of the progress we have made to support ongoing investments in the comprehensive literacy system. Funds are allocated for replenishing the guided reading book room collection of more than 2,500 titles, representing appropriate texts for readers from kindergarten through fifth grade. In addition, we finance a set of core professional texts as lesson and professional development touchstones for each new teacher according to grade level. Sending groups of teachers to national literacy conferences to stay abreast of cutting-edge research and proven practice is an administrative and budgetary priority.

Time frames and expectations for literacy assessment and response systems are now a scheduled part of every year and every grade, along with pacing guides to orchestrate a mutual tempo and curricular attention. The teachers' association contract includes a provision for a half day of professional release time to ensure that all data from the Language Arts Assessment System are entered in a timely manner and ready for generating data reports for collaborative groups to set measurable reading goals. The database places ten years of longitudinal data at the fingertips of teachers, interventionists, and administrators.

Over the course of many years, new role positions have evolved to facilitate ongoing improvements. Where reading teachers used to work in isolation from one another and from classroom aims, we now have a safety net team of reading intervention teachers as a collaborative think tank to address the needs of struggling readers in tiers of intervention support. Their new responsibilities encompass in-class supports, short-term pullout groupings, and educational consultations with classroom teachers. Instead of sending students to specialists to be "fixed," the interventionist's role centers on integrated learning targets aiming to achieve reading and writing success in the classroom. The literacy coordinator position gradually evolved due to pleas from the classroom teachers to the principal and to the director of educational programs. As enthusiasm for the instructional frameworks of reading or writing workshop pressed forward, teachers requested constant and accessible support for implementing the quality instruction that has become our hallmark.

Professional development options, in every shape and size, now populate our monthly calendars. Teacher-led study groups crop up more frequently. And educational topics to investigate are coordinated with district and building goals. We're capturing exemplary literacy instruction on digital video to develop our own footage for training new teachers and for reflecting on our practice.

It is satisfying to look back and take stock of the strides we have made toward aligning systems and unifying intentions at Moreland Hills. Structures and routines provide a framework for continuing our work in refining and augmenting our comprehensive literacy system.

We cannot rest on our laurels. As with house improvements, Moreland Hills' comprehensive literacy system has a growing list of repairs and renovations. I and the literacy team have some aspirations in mind.

We need to review and refine the assessments and documentation. These have endured yearly refinements. Now that we have instituted some midyear assessments in reading, writing, and word study, perhaps we could add those scores to the database. The added midyear data could help us improve our monitoring and reporting systems. Agreeing on specific data comparisons for our technology department to organize into timely data reports could stimulate faculty dialogue at critical points in the year, helping us identify trends and measure the impact of our actions. I wonder how we might further support the routine use of data and observations to make instructional decisions.

More work needs to be done to empower our students to actively take part in maximizing their achievement. If we phrase our essential learnings into student-friendly "I can" statements, as recommended by assessment specialist Richard Stiggins et al. (2004), we can more directly engage students' participation in targeting personal academic goals, then further empower them to track academic progress with student data files and graphs. In addition, we could rework our grade-level writing rubrics into student-friendly formats and consistently use the rubrics for providing descriptive feedback to young writers. The issues raised by disjointed grading systems also vie for imminent attention. We need to develop consistent grading criteria that communicate achievement performance on instructional targets more than averaging percentage points on variable class assignments, homework, and tissue box contributions. Setting plain and common criteria for report card grades reinforces the targets for learning in the eyes of students, teachers, and parents.

We must widen the circle of our comprehensive literacy response plan to include parents as partners. How might we invite parents into the conversation and increase our capacity to respond to the issues they raise as barriers to student success? Parents represent diverse points of view that need to be heard. We could learn a lot from one another about ways to adjust our practice and to extend a common language.

As we continue to reap the rewards of an integrated and informed literacy vision for kindergarten through fifth grade, we are challenged to consider ways to extend continuity into our middle school. The needs of adolescent readers and the unique schedules and conditions of a middle school environment call for a shift from the elementary school model in the implementation of literacy instruction and systems of support. Adolescent literacy requires new initiatives, perhaps using similar processes. Bridging success to our middle school and high school raises fresh opportunities for collaboration and innovation.

Together, our teachers, principals, and parents will continue to set yearly goals to sharpen our focus to support literacy achievement for every child.

Investing in Continuous Improvement

Continuous improvement is precisely that. As Shari Lewis and Lamb Chop sang, "This is the song that never ends." Bold actions produce fresh challenges and give rise to additional great ideas and applications. Just when your staff is satisfied with the selection of common assessments the "to do" list grows like a weed. Next you'll need to plan training sessions for administering the tests, generate notebooks or web pages posting instructions and forms, and design a database or documentation routine so the data gathered can be analyzed to inform decisions. Each initiative to align systems causes a domino effect of necessary professional education and support, resource development, new roles and responsibilities, or endless refinements. So, why even embark on this journey? Why begin a process that will never be completed? Is it worth the investment of time, effort, and money?

Continuous improvement is not about us. It is for the children. It is not about the amount of work or how long it will take to get it right. As elementary educators, our daily decisions affect young lives for many years into the future. Whether intentionally or inadvertently, our words and actions influence a child's self-identity as a learner and as a contributor to the world. That is true of the classroom teacher and it is true of the system itself. We owe it to the children to interconnect systems of support and empowerment for learning. We need to reinvent educational systems to efficiently and effectively maximize the learning for every child. And we cannot do it with isolated spurts or disconnected programs.

The most successful organizations are structured to absorb innovation quickly and efficiently. They elicit continuous feedback from stakeholders, review effectiveness of current practice, and pilot fresh solutions even before every detail is perfected. Microsoft did not generate success by securing and defending the status quo. With the agility of professional basketball players, successful organizations are nimbly poised to shift into action in response to observed circumstances. They remain both flexible and receptive to change.

The success of continuous improvement plans depends on the dual agents of sustainability and flexibility. At first glance, these two appear to be opposing ideals. Sustainability relates to things that are steadfast and lasting. Flexibility conjures images of frequent shifting and changing. The primary focus for developing your comprehensive literacy system should be to create a sustainable culture that routinely aims at challenging the status quo. What remain steadfast and sure are the system-wide habits. Customs such as seeking a continuous loop of feedback among role groups, monitoring student progress to inform our effectiveness, and empowering internal opportunities for professional study all signal a readiness for change.

Change is assured—in life and especially in schools. It is inevitable that shifts in technology will redefine what it means to be literate. What constitutes best practice will not remain a static list of instructional features. Updates in research will further refine our understanding of how best to affect growth and achievement. In response to the unavoidable change in our communities, our state, and our world, we need to create sustainable systems that are pliable enough to shift with the changing needs, yet structured enough to maintain a sharp unified focus on maximizing student learning.

Developing a successful comprehensive literacy system is not about finally getting it perfect; it's about creating a unified organization with habits and disciplines that orchestrate a heightened communal impact on student success. It means engaging a continuous cycle of review and adjustment as our newest professional knowledge informs our good intentions. Remember: Today's solutions are the tentative strongholds grounded by our current best thinking.

Appendixes

Appendix A

The following is a list of professional texts and resources we provide for every classroom teacher, according to the grade taught, in support of quality instructional design for reading workshop, writing workshop, and developmental word study. These texts are budgeted in lieu of commercial teachers' manuals, basal series, or instructional programs.

Kindergarten

Guided Reading: Good First Teaching for All Children by Fountas and Pinnell (Heinemann)
Interactive Writing and Interactive Editing by Swartz, Klein, and Shook (Dominie Press)
Phonics Lessons by Fountas and Pinnell (Heinemann)
Reading with Meaning by Miller (Stenhouse)
Units of Study for Primary Writing by Calkins (Heinemann)

First Grade

Guided Reading: Good First Teaching for All Children by Fountas and Pinnell (Heinemann)
Interactive Writing and Interactive Editing by Swartz, Klein, and Shook (Dominie Press)
Reading with Meaning by Miller (Stenhouse)
Reading with Strategies (Stage 1) (Celebration Press)
Units of Study for Primary Writing by Calkins (Heinemann)
Word Journeys by Ganske (Guilford Press)

Second Grade

Guiding Readers and Writers: Grades 3–6 by Fountas and Pinnell (Heinemann)
Reading with Meaning by Miller (Stenhouse)
Reading with Strategies (Stage 2) (Celebration Press)
Units of Study for Primary Writing by Calkins (Heinemann)
Word Journeys by Ganske (Guilford Press)

Third Grade

Guiding Readers and Writers: Grades 3–6 by Fountas and Pinnell (Heinemann)
Strategies That Work by Harvey and Goudvis (Stenhouse)
Teaching the Qualities of Writing by Fletcher and Portalupi (Heinemann)
Word Journeys by Ganske (Guilford Press)

Fourth Grade

Guiding Readers and Writers: Grades 3–6 by Fountas and Pinnell (Heinemann)
Strategies That Work by Harvey and Goudvis (Stenhouse)
Teaching the Qualities of Writing by Fletcher and Portalupi (Heinemann)
Word Journeys by Ganske (Guilford Press)

Fifth Grade

Guiding Readers and Writers: Grades 3–6 by Fountas and Pinnell (Heinemann)
Strategies That Work by Harvey and Goudvis (Stenhouse)
Teaching the Qualities of Writing by Fletcher and Portalupi (Heinemann)
Word Journeys by Ganske (Guilford Press)

Appendix B

CRITIQUE OF READING ASSESSMENTS

ASSESSMENT	FOR WHICH GRADE LEVEL(S)?	STATE READING INDICATORS ASSESSED	USER-FRIENDLY FOR KIDS?	USER-FRIENDLY FOR CLASSROOM TEACHERS?	TRAINING NEEDED FOR STANDARDIZED ADMINISTRATION	COMMENTS

ASSESSMENT	FOR WHICH GRADE LEVEL(S)?	STATE WRITING INDICATORS ASSESSED	USER-FRIENDLY FOR KIDS?	USER-FRIENDLY FOR CLASSROOM TEACHERS?	TRAINING NEEDED FOR STANDARDIZED ADMINISTRATION	COMMENTS

Appendix C

DESCRIPTION AND REFERENCES FOR SELECTED COMMON ASSESSMENTS

Assessing Reading Level

Moreland Hills Elementary School requires the use of specific assessments to determine students' reading levels and to assess reading fluency, accuracy, and comprehension to match children to appropriate texts. Kindergartners are assessed at the end of the year and first- through fifth-grade students are assessed at the beginning and end of the year. The Developmental Reading Assessment is used for kindergarten through beginning third-grade readers and the Qualitative Reading Assessment is used at the end of third grade through grade five.

Developmental Reading Assessment (Pearson Learning Group)

Students read from a colorful library of leveled texts as the teacher observes and documents individual reading behaviors. An appropriate level for reading instruction can be identified based on criteria for reading fluency, comprehension, and accuracy.

Beaver, Joetta. 2001. *Developmental Reading Assessment, K–3*. 1st ed. Parsippany, NJ: Celebration Press.

Qualitative Reading Inventory (Allyn and Bacon)

This collection of leveled passages, narratives and expositories, is accompanied by questions that assess a reader's explicit and implicit comprehension. Teachers can note reading behaviors as they listen to each reader and determine an approximate level for each student's reading instruction.

Leslie, Lauren, and JoAnne Caldwell. 2000. *Qualitative Reading Inventory–4 (4th edition)*. Boston: Allyn and Bacon.

Developmental Spelling Analysis

Students' knowledge of specific spelling features are quickly and easily assessed to determine the stage of spelling development of any particular student using a series of stage-related spelling lists.

Ganske, Kathy. 2000. *Word Journeys: Assessment-Guided Phonics, Spelling, and Vocabulary Instruction.* New York: Guilford Press.

Writing Prompt Tasks for Grades 1–5

At each grade level, Moreland Hills teachers have designed a prompted writing task, supported first by a graphic organizer, administered under common conditions and within the same week in April. Tasks prompt for writing in a genre that is linked to the state indicators for each grade (i.e., personal narrative, descriptive writing, business letter).

Fry Word Lists

Lists of twenty-five words at a time that represent the most commonly used words are given to students in first and second grades to assess and monitor sight word recognition.

Fry, E., J. Kress, and D. Fountoukidis. 2004. *The Reading Teacher's Book of Lists*. Englewood Cliffs, NJ: Prentice Hall.

Fry, E. B. 1980. "The New Instant Word List." *The Reading Teacher* 34:284–290.

Grade-Level "Snap Words"

Grade-level teams generated lists of common words that students are expected to spell correctly "in a snap." The lists are cumulative, beginning with the "Kindergarten Top 14" words and adding more to each grade through fourth grade. Students are periodically assessed for spelling these words in trimester increments and are kept accountable for applying accurate spelling of mastered snap words in final writing drafts.

Letter ID Task

Students are given a page of scrambled capital and lowercase letters. The teacher records observations of known, confused, or unknown letters and documents other notable behaviors.

Clay, Marie. 1993. *An Observation Survey of Early Literacy Achievement*. Portsmouth, NH: Heinemann.

Sentence Dictation Task

In small groups of students with similar reading levels, teachers read a dictated sentence for students to record on a blank sheet of paper. The score is determined by the number of appropriate phonemes represented in the student's writing of that sentence. Behaviors are noted.

Clay, Marie. 1993. *An Observation Survey of Early Literacy Achievement*. Portsmouth, NH: Heinemann.

Concepts of Print Task

Each teacher reads a familiar common book to individual students, asking the student to frame a letter, frame a word, indicate where to start reading, point to the words being read, or tell the meaning of punctuation such as a period, question mark, and exclamation point at designated points in the text. The teacher notes the child's command of general book knowledge.

Appendix D

Reading Workshop

Mosaic of Thought, second edition, by Zimmermann and Keene (Heinemann)

The Art of Teaching Reading by Calkins (Longman)

Seven Keys to Comprehension by Zimmermann and Hutchins

Guided Reading: Good First Teaching for All Children by Fountas and Pinnell (Heinemann)

Guiding Readers and Writers, Grades 3–6 by Fountas and Pinnell (Heinemann)

On Solid Ground by Taberski (Heinemann)

Growing Readers: Units of Study in the Primary Classroom by Collins (Stenhouse)

Reading with Meaning by Miller (Stenhouse)

Strategies That Work, second edition, by Harvey and Goudvis (Stenhouse)

In the Company of Children by Hindley (Stenhouse)

Writing Workshop

Craft Lessons: Teaching Writing K–8 by Fletcher and Portalupi (Stenhouse)

Nonfiction Craft Lessons: Teaching Information Writing K–8 by Fletcher and Portalupi (Stenhouse)

Teaching the Qualities of Writing by Fletcher and Portalupi (Heinemann)

Notebook Know-How: Strategies for the Writer's Notebook by Buckner (Stenhouse)

The No-Nonsense Guide to Teaching Writing by Davis and Hill (Heinemann)

How's It Going? by Anderson (Heinemann)

In the Company of Children by Hindley (Stenhouse)

Developmental Word Study

Words Their Way: Word Study for Phonics, Vocabulary, and Spelling Instruction by Bear, Invernizzi, Templeton, and Johnston (Pearson Prentice Hall)

Words Their Way: Letter and Picture Sorts for Emergent Spellers by Bear, Invernizzi, Johnston, and Templeton (Pearson Prentice Hall)

Words Their Way: Word Sorts for Letter Name–Alphabetic Spellers by Johnston, Invernizzi, Bear, and Templeton (Pearson Prentice Hall)

Words Their Way: Word Sorts for Within Word Pattern Spellers by Invernizzi, Johnston, and Bear (Pearson Prentice Hall)

Words Their Way: Word Sorts for Syllables and Affixes Spellers by Johnston, Invernizzi, and Bear (Pearson Prentice Hall)

Words Their Way: Word Sorts for Derivational Relations Spellers by Templeton, Johnston, Bear, and Invernizzi (Pearson Prentice Hall)

Word Journeys: Assessment-Guided Phonics, Spelling, and Vocabulary Instruction by Ganske (Guilford Press)

The Great Word Catalogue by Ohanian (Heinemann)

Appendix E

SKILLS/STRATEGIES: A BANK OF CLASSROOM ACCOMMODATIONS

IF A STUDENT...	THEN...

Appendix F-1

EMERGENT SKILLS/STRATEGIES: A BANK OF CLASSROOM ACCOMMODATIONS

Adapted from Moreland Hills Elementary School Teachers' Literacy Response Plan by Maren Koepf, 2007.

IF A STUDENT...	THEN...
Lacks verbal phonological awareness: * Rhyming * Blending Sounds * Isolating Sounds	Use assessment to identify focus for phonological awareness Expose to nursery rhymes and other poems and chants with much rhythm and rhyme Provide opportunities for repeated listening to songs, poems, and chants Practice choral "reading" of familiar song lyrics, poems, chants, refrains Play "Guess My Word," segmenting sounds of a single-syllable word Use Elkonin sound boxes, pushing tokens for each sound in single-syllable words Clap the rhythm of first and last names to hear syllables Play "I spy something that rhymes with..." Use picture cards or sets of items for initial and final sound isolation
Lacks flexible/instant letter recognition	Practice letter recognition tasks with a variety of fonts, sizes, or mediums Match upper- and lowercase pairs Create scavenger hunts, locating and tagging letters within known texts or around the room Read alphabet books Make/read alphabet books and letter books Practice 1:1 pointing while "reading" the alphabet, varying the line breaks ABC ABCDEFG DEF HIJK Locate letter shapes found in the environment Play computer games focusing on letter recognition Sort magnetic letters or letter tiles by physical attributes (lines, tunnels, circles, color, etc.) Create activities with letter puzzles, sandpaper letters, shaving cream, clay, Wikki Stix, etc. Read and point to the letter sequences on the name chart or on the ABC chart
Lacks flexible/instant letter formation	Play "flash 'n' write": Using letter cards, flash a letter for student to name; cover it while student quickly forms the letter; check the card against the formed letter Explicitly teach sets of letters that have the same starting spot (r,n,m) Practice starting spots and verbalizing the formation path: "Around the loop, up, up, and down = d" Provide multiple opportunities to trace letters, using the correct starting spot Provide opportunities to form letters using whole-body positions (with a partner, as needed)

IF A STUDENT...	THEN...
Does not understand that letters represent sounds	Assess to find out which letters are recognized and which, if any, letter-sound associations are known
	Work on two or three distinctly different sounds at a time
	Provide opportunities for letter-picture sorts and letter-object sorts
	Create collages of magazine photos representing a given sound
	Start with the letters whose names begin with the sound (B, D, J, K, P, T, V, Z)
	Work on two or three distinctly different sounds at a time
	Play "I spy something that begins with..."
	Play matching games and memory games with letters and pictures
	Make books labeling pictures, all with the same starting sound
	Assign one letter on which to become an expert (its sound, shape, what it reminds you of, how your mouth is formed to make that sound)
	Routinely practice reciting the key word pictures to the ABC chart
	Pick an object, make its initial letter in a variety of mediums (clay, chalk, crayon)
	Paint a large consonant, and surround it with pictures of things that start with it
	Practiced shared and interactive writing of labels, signs, messages, warnings, modeling the isolation of the first sound and writing the letter for that sound
Lacks background knowledge and expressive vocabulary for common objects, animals, story language, and concepts	Respond and converse with the child in complete sentences
	Provide opportunities for dramatic play in small groups (possible themes: store, post office, bus, home)
	Provide many opportunities for time at the listening station
	Read aloud books with playful refrains for shared reading
	Allow for buddy reading of big books and poems that have been frequently read aloud in shared reading
	Read aloud nonfiction texts at appropriate developmental levels; discuss concepts modeling vocabulary
	Create simple caption books around topics such as food, recess, friends, tools, school, labeling the nouns
	Read and talk about books, characters, expressions of characters, details in the pictures, actions, predictions from the pictures, and areas of interest or connections
	Facilitate conversations about the details of field trips by taking photos; comment on discoveries as well as feelings
	Encourage participation in show and tell
	Read and think aloud about different versions of the same story or topic

IF A STUDENT...	THEN...
Does not locate known words in flexible contexts/fonts	Teach only one or two words per week or month (as needed)
	Provide individualized word card rings of the words they know
	Teach the student how to visualize the word
	Have the student practice writing the word in different mediums
	Take a word card on a scavenger hunt around the room (look on charts, poems, books)
	Highlight the given word within photocopied texts
	Have the student count the number of times the word appears in a given text
	After a shared reading, have students use a framing card to locate the given word
	Have the student build the word using magnetic letters, then write it
Confuses or is unfamiliar with print terminology such as *word / letter, capital / lowercase, period / question mark*	Have the student construct his/her name in magnetic letters; explain the difference between word and letter
	After shared reading, have the student frame one letter or two letters
	After shared reading, have the student frame one word or two words
	Provide a sentence strip of a short dictated sentence; have student count the words
	Provide a sentence strip of a short dictated sentence; have the student count the letters
	Have the student highlight specific items (period, spaces, capital letters, tall letters, etc.) on a short poem
	Have the student discriminate between two words beginning with the same sound, a long word, and a short word by matching the pictures (such as bat/banana or hippopotamus/hat)
	Have student highlight periods in a poem
Confuses left-to-right directionality on the word or text level	When reading aloud to a student, think aloud about where you start to read each page and how to move down the page
	When reading aloud to the student, ask, "Where do I start to read?"
	Use a green "start" dot at the beginning of a sentence and a red "stop" dot at the end
	Have the student "read" the alphabet chart or name chart; point left to right across the chart
	When reading familiar labels in the room or in a book, have the student slide a finger under the letters of the word from left to right
	Have the student locate the first letter of a word in a variety of texts
	Have the student sort letters daily, focusing on ones where directionality is confused

IF A STUDENT...	THEN...
Does not demonstrate crisp 1:1 pointing/matching	Demonstrate the task by pointing to and naming objects, pictures, or familiar words
	Have the student use an extended pointer (drinking straw, chopstick, unsharpened pencil)
	Consider the font size, spacing, and placement of text when selecting books for the student
	Have the student assemble a cut-up dictated sentence and reread while pointing
	Prompt for voice-text matching:
	"Did your voice match the words you see?"
	"Did you have enough words on that page to match what you said?"
	"You said... [repeat how child read it as you point]. That didn't match. Read it again to make your voice match the words."
Does not recall information from stories read aloud	Use an interactive format during read-aloud (stop periodically to ask questions and share responses during reading)
	Have the student describe what he/she pictures after hearing a piece of text read
	Stop at points in a read-aloud to have students illustrate what is happening so far
	Have students reenact part of the story

Appendix F–2

EARLY SKILLS/STRATEGIES: A BANK OF CLASSROOM ACCOMMODATIONS

Adapted from Moreland Hills Elementary School Teachers' Literacy Response Plan by Maren Koepf, 2007.

IF A STUDENT...	THEN...
Does not demonstrate routine left-to-right directionality	Explicitly model 1:1 pointing while reading aloud, thinking aloud for return sweep, left page before right page, and looking left to right across new words
	Ask student to point to where the reader should start to read
	Use big books or enlarged poems to demonstrate left-to-right reading
	Arrange magnetic letters in ABC order and have the student use a pointer to name the letters
	Arrange magnetic letters in ABC order, varying the lines of print in vertical groupings: ABCD EFG...
	Create a board game where the pawns move along a path from left to right, top to bottom
	Have the student "read" the alphabet chart, with a pointer, moving from left to right
	Have student drop and count pennies into egg cartons or other grid-molded containers, left to right
Does not routinely demonstrate crisp 1:1 match, pointing under each word	Have the student point 1:1 while the teacher points above the text
	Consider the font size, spacing, and placement of text in books read by student
	Prompt during reading: "Did your voice match the words you see?" "Did you have enough words to match what you said?" "You said ... [repeat exactly as the child read it]. That didn't match. Read it again to make your voice match the words."
	Have the student point to and name objects and/or known words to demonstrate the task
	Have the student use an extended pointer (e.g., pencil eraser, drinking straw, etc.)
	Generate a short sentence with the student; cut apart the words; have student reassemble
	Generate short story dictated by the child; reread with 1:1 pointing.
Does not locate words based on the first letter/sound	Place label cards to match pictures or items (based on first letter sound)
	Sort words/pictures based on first letter
	Use a masking card to isolate the first letter of a word in text
	During book introduction ask student to predict and locate an unfamiliar word based on the first letter. Prompt: "What letter would you expect to see at the beginning of...?"
	Assemble cut-up sentences
	Play "I spy something that starts with... [letter]."
	Gather items that begin with the given letter (scavenger hunt)
	Play "I spy something that begins with... [letter]," looking at pages in alphabet book
	Read/create alphabet books
	Photocopy a short text with pictures; with child, highlight initial sound of key words (nouns) and the picture that gives the clue for that word

IF A STUDENT...	THEN...
Does not locate or monitor for known sight words embedded in texts OR Retains limited recognition of appropriate sight words	Focus on overlearning only 5 words per week based on the Fry (high-frequency word list) Have student write known words in a variety of mediums (clay, sand, chalk, etc.) During a book introduction, ask the student to frame and name words being learned When a student stops at a known word, say, "You know that word." Find opportunities to make connections between what words child knows in writing/reading Create sentences or phrases using sight word tiles Use framing cards to locate and read 3–4 sight words in familiar texts and big books Play "flash 'n' write": Flash a word for student to read; cover it as student writes it or makes it in magnetic letters; student checks his or her written word against the word card Play "my pile/your pile": Flash word cards (no more than 5–7) to student; student must name the word in a couple of seconds to keep a card in his or her pile Use visualization techniques to draw student's attention to hard-to-remember features Have student name and sort words based on number of letters, initial letter, known/challenging Practice and graph the number of high-frequency phrase cards the student can read in 2 minutes

Does not stop and notice when meaning breaks down	**Before reading**
	
	Consider the book selection. Is it just right for the student to access vocabulary and concepts?
	
	Give a strong and supportive book introduction telling the full gist of the story and giving practice with saying some of the unusual language or phrasing
	
	Engage student in a picture walk
	
	During reading
	
	Teacher should avoid overmonitoring for the student. Allow the student to notice and correct
	
	Prompt for strategic thinking:
	
	    "You said...Did that make sense? Read it again to make sense."
	
	    "Stop and think about what you read."
	
	    "Is that what it said?"
	
	    "Try that again."
	
	Tell child to look at the picture for clues
	
	Cover the text before the student reads a given page and ask student to predict what will happen on that page (don't cover the picture)
	
	Encourage student's predictions, connections, and visualizations
	
	Periodically have student write or tell what is happening in the story so far
	
	Teach the "click or clunk" fix-up strategy for monitoring confusions and taking specific action
	
	Explicitly repeat, "Everything you read should make sense to you"
	
	Let the student arrange sentence strips in logical sequence

IF A STUDENT...	THEN...
Does not stop and monitor when the sentence structure doesn't sound right	Select books that are within the student's oral language abilities; consider unfamiliar language structures when planning book introductions
	Invite the student to repeat selected language structures during the book introduction
	Catch moments when the student does stop, then explicitly praise the behavior with "Good. You noticed that didn't sound right. What else can you try there?"
	Prompt for listening to the sound of the sentence structure or language:
	"You said [tell the word]. Is that how we would say it?" "Read that again and make it sound right."
	"Did that sound right?" "Read that again and make it sound right."
	At difficulty...
	Prompt for rereading:
	"Read that again and think of a word that would sound right (or fit) there."
	"Read that again and try a word that makes sense and sounds right here."
	"Would [tell the word] fit there?"
	Use cloze passages during text reading (covering some key words with white correction tape)
Frequently appeals for help; gives up easily	Teacher should be cautious of jumping in too quickly and teaching helplessness
	Set an expectation that student initiate some problem-solving before being helped
	Prompt for initiative:
	"Try it."
	"Could it be...or...?" (supply two choices)
	"What do you know that can help you solve that word?"
	"Show me a part you know in that word."
	Use a bookmark illustrating strategies you have practiced. Ask student to pick one and try it
	Educate parents about possible prompts that encourage problem-solving

IF A STUDENT...	THEN...
Lacks appropriate phrasing and fluency	Model the difference between word-by-word and fluent phrasing
	Model variety of intonations and adjusted reading rates
	Provide opportunities for repeated rereadings:
	* To prepare for reading to a small audience
	* To record
	* Reader's theater
	* Practice the text to become an "expert" on that text
	* Create a poetry collection to read and reread to partners or whole group
	* Shared reading of familiar texts and refrains
	Practice choral reading
	Practice echo reading
	Find texts with refrain and some repetition
	Once the student easily attends to print, encourage reading without pointing 1:1 to every word
	Glide a masking card along the text from left to right to encourage eye movement across text
	Provide many opportunities for reading lots of easier, familiar texts
	Photocopy a passage and mark the natural phrases with slash marks
Misreads punctuation, affecting comprehension	Teach punctuation as road signs
	Explain explicitly how the author uses punctuation marks to signal how to read a passage
	Demonstrate how a reader's voice changes with different punctuation marks
	Practice intonation with echo reading: Teacher reads and student repeats the phrase, sentence, or paragraph
	Photocopy a passage, eliminating punctuation; show how punctuation placement affects reading

IF A STUDENT...	THEN...
Does not apply flexible decoding strategies	Teach that there are 3 kinds of words: 1. The kind you know/recognize in a snap (sight words) 2. The kind you can slide across slowly and read ("sound out") 3. The kind that remind you of a known word or word part (using analogy like can—man) Teach students to mask off familiar affixes (-ed, -ing) Provide an "at-a-glance" personal word wall for the student to add to and reference during reading/writing Provide word sorts in which students search for specific features Write word on a whiteboard and demonstrate how to chunk familiar clusters across a longer word **Word Wall Activities:** Present activities that create familiarity with common word parts (rimes, blends, affixes) Teach how to make analogies to known words and model how to notice familiar word parts in text Play "Guess My Word," giving one clue at a time to reveal the mystery word from the word wall
Presents many misconceptions regarding literal information	Give more supportive book introductions, including names of characters and unusual book language atypical to conversation Check comprehension more frequently with mini-conferences on shorter portions of text Set a specific purpose before reading: focus on one story element at a time Use story maps and graphic organizers of story elements: characters, setting, problem, solution Practice the strategy of visualizing as you go, sharing quick sketches or verbal descriptions Model and practice returning to text to locate information that answers a literal ("right there") question Teach student to find the 5 W's (who, what, when, where, why)
Typically does not recall events or details in sequential order	Model and practice verbally retelling the beginning, middle, and end of a familiar story Have student sequence sentence strips or pictures telling a familiar story Photocopy a short story to be cut into chunks of text and sequenced Photocopy a story and have student highlight signal words that indicate sequence Play memory games sequencing objects, books, numbers, or events of the day Scaffold verbal retellings with signal words: *first, next, then, finally* Link sequencing to summarizing small portions of the text "as you go"
Does not make predictions for plausible outcomes	Give guided practice in making predictions based on illustrations, title, and background knowledge Think aloud to model making multiple predictions based on clues and background knowledge Think aloud to model making predictions and revising them based on new evidence from the story

Appendix F–3

DEVELOPING SKILLS/STRATEGIES: A BANK OF CLASSROOM ACCOMMODATIONS

Adapted from Moreland Hills Elementary School Teachers' Literacy Response Plan by Maren Koepf, 2007.

IF A STUDENT...	THEN...
Avoids or resists reading	Seek student's interests; administer an interest inventory
	Help student with ways to self-select books ("just right," read blurb on back, author's notes, first few paragraphs)
	Celebrate successes; comment explicitly about the strategies observed
	Lighten the workload (shorter texts, shared reading with a buddy, fewer extensions or questions)
	Set the student up for success; teach the student what he/she needs to know to be successful
	Set a goal with the student
	Try mysteries, humor, nonfiction, or author series to pique interest
	Instruct at independent level for a period of time to build confidence
	Confer more frequently and check on reading accuracy/fluency/comprehension
	Graph the number of books/pages/passages read each week/month
	Spend more time talking informally about books (book talks or book recommendations)
	Respond more frequently to student journal entries about books/reading
	Engage the student in a book club with peers
Does not have a strategy for systematically decoding polysyllabic words	Model how to divide words
	Use a whiteboard to segment a word for the student; have the student do this
	Have student build new words with more complex rimes (-atch, -ight, -ound)
	Systematically build familiarity with common prefixes and suffixes
	Systematically teach basic word principles
	Show the student how to mask prefixes and suffixes with a finger in the text
	Have the student cut words apart from word strips
	Write the word on a paper and have student circle/highlight familiar parts/clusters
Does not reread to deepen understanding	Use a think-aloud to model self-questioning and how rereading supports having questions answered
	Make sure texts are at an appropriate level and interest to the student
	Provide more supportive book introductions to build background knowledge
	Have student write questions about the text/topic in a response journal. Teach how to go back in the text to locate the answers to one's own questions
	During discussion of the text, find opportunities to return to the text for evidence or to listen again to the author's use of words
	Prompt the student to ask questions ("Does this make sense to me?" "Is this what I thought would happen?" "Does this remind me of something I have experienced?")

IF A STUDENT...	THEN...
Does not efficiently scan text for key information (to answer questions and/or to locate supportive evidence)	Set a specific purpose for reading based on genre, structure, interests, predictions
	Teach the student to read questions first to help set a purpose
	Have the student recall the general sequence of what has already been read and segment the passage into sections to search (narrow the field)
	Have student highlight key words in text that link to the question
	Teach the student to notice signal words (*first, next, in addition, finally, in conclusion*)
	Teach students to use nonfiction text features to help locate information
	Teach students to anticipate the answer and possible words/phrases to scan for
Does not use nonfiction text features to gather information before and during reading	Model how different text features are used to help make meaning in the text
	Have the student locate specific text features across a variety of informational texts and build familiarity with what each provides
	Have student write captions, make a table of contents, generate graphs and charts for books that don't have them or for books created on a topic of interest
	Provide a more in-depth book introduction to include the layout of nonfiction features
Does not recognize specific nonfiction text structures to help set purpose for reading	Introduce six text structures and their attributes, showing specific examples (descriptive, chronological, problem-solution, compare/contrast, question/answer, cause/effect)
	Have students work in pairs to generate six sentences on one topic representing each structure
	Create an anchor chart of signal words associated with each structure
	Using a stack of nonfiction texts, have student groups label the text structure with sticky notes and give evidence (attributes and/or signal words)
	Have students use graphic organizers matched to each text structure to take notes
	Read aloud nonfiction text and think aloud about what structure the text might be and why
	Before reading nonfiction, have students anticipate the content based on the identified structure
Does not discern important information from interesting details	Explicitly teach nonfiction features that signal importance (boldface, different fonts, captions, labels, headings, charts, diagrams, bullets, definitions...)
	Teach cue words and phrases that signal importance (i.e., *for example, for instance, in fact, in conclusion, most important, such as, therefore, but, on the other hand*)
	Have student code texts for information that is important (I), interesting (*), surprising (!)
	Have student use two-column note-taking forms while reading (to sort Interesting/Important, Big Ideas/Little Ideas, etc.)
	For fiction, teach the student to identify the 4 key elements of story (important characters, setting, problem or goal, solution) to discern where important information will be found

IF A STUDENT...	THEN...
Does not easily identify the main idea	Practice with a detailed picture to identify the whole idea versus the details
	Link important details together; name the way they connect as the main idea
	Teach the student to look at the beginning or end of a passage or paragraph to locate the topic sentence
	Have the student locate the big idea or topic sentence from a paragraph and highlight it
	Have the student identify titles for paragraphs, chapters, or articles
	Cut titles off short articles; have students match them up
	Teach students to list a sequence of key words and write a summary statement
Does not identify details that support a main idea	Match or sort details with or from main ideas
	Use appropriate graphic organizers to organize details and main ideas (fishbone, web, hamburger)
	Teach the student to sort the right answer from a close answer (test-taking strategy)
	Teach the student to sort "important" from "unimportant" details
	Teach the student to locate key words and cross out unnecessary information in a short piece of text
	Discuss a story or text and teach the student how to revisit the text for details
Does not gather and sustain information across longer texts	Have the student stop at appropriate points during reading to recount what is happening before reading on
	Link summarizing to sequencing "as you go" with each portion of the text
	Have the student do a "quick write" for one minute after each portion of the text (chapter, heading, etc.)
	Have student do a "quick draw" (fast sketch showing character/action) after each chapter or segment
Does not comprehend vocabulary or terminology basic to the text, plot, or meaning	Demonstrate and practice strategies for inferring meaning from context clues
	Directly teach vocabulary related to the topic or important to the story
	Use the same terminology across grades as is used on high-stakes assessments
	Have students sort phrases or words under category headings
	Assign student to analyze important vocabulary words when responding to texts (e.g., choose 4 words from the text and write a synonym or antonym for each, record related characteristics, and illustrate each word)
	Give the student opportunities for listening to rich literature
	Assign concept sorts using phrases and/or pictures
Does not effectively summarize the gist of the text	Model and assign a graphic organizer that includes Somebody...Wanted....But...So
	Share a variety of book jacket blurbs and discuss the purpose and how they are written
	Have student write a book jacket with the blurb summarizing the text on the back
	Demonstrate on a short article how to summarize pieces in 15 words or less
	Teach students to use a note card for summaries and a sheet of paper for retellings
	Teach the student to tell the 5 W's: who, what, where, when, why

IF A STUDENT...	THEN...
Does not infer meaning (theme, humor, generalizations, time shifts, characterizations, symbolism, etc.)	Have the student practice "reading between the lines" from pictures; what can the student tell about the setting (era, season, place) and characters' emotions?
	Teach the student QAR (question-answer relationships); have student learn to identify "right there" literal answers vs. "you and the author" inferential answers
	Have the student practice inferring from phrases (the clue from the text as well as the clue in his or her head)
	Model how to make predictions and confirm or adjust them "as you go," citing evidence or phrases from the text
	Provide practice figuring out new vocabulary in context based on the surrounding words

Appendix G

LITERACY RESPONSE PLAN

Student or Group: _____ Classroom Teacher: _____ Date of Plan: _____

Specialist(s) Consulted: _____ Date(s): _____

A. Targeted Goal: _____

Intervention Commitment: (Select from "If...Then" menu)

(1)_____

(2)_____

Date: Date: Date: Comments/Observations:

_____   _____   _____

_____   _____   _____

_____   _____   _____

_____   _____   _____

B. Targeted Goal: _____

Intervention Commitment: (Select from "If...Then" menu)

(1)_____

(2)_____

Date: Date: Date: Comments/Observations:

_____   _____   _____

_____   _____   _____

_____   _____   _____

_____   _____   _____

References

Ainsworth, Larry, and Donald Viegut. 2006. *Common Formative Assessments: How to Connect Standards-Based Instruction and Assessment.* Thousand Oaks, CA: Corwin.

Allington, Richard L. 2004. "Setting the Record Straight." *Educational Leadership* 61 (6): 22–25.

———. 2005. "What Counts as Evidence in Evidence-Based Education." *Reading Today* 3 (3): 16.

———. 2006. *What Really Matters for Struggling Readers: Designing Research-Based Programs.* New York: Pearson Education.

Allington, Richard L., and Peter H. Johnston, eds. 2002. *Reading to Learn: Lessons from Exemplary Fourth-Grade Classrooms.* New York: Guilford.

Anderson, Carl. 2000. *How's It Going? A Practical Guide to Conferring with Student Writers.* Portsmouth, NH: Heinemann.

Atwell, Nancie. 1998. *In the Middle: New Understandings About Writing, Reading, and Learning.* 2nd ed. Portsmouth, NH: Heinemann.

———. 2002. *Lessons That Change Writers.* Portsmouth, NH: Heinemann.

Bear, Donald, Marcia Invernizzi, Shane R. Templeton, and Francine Johnston. 2000. *Words Their Way: Word Study for Phonics, Vocabulary, and Spelling Instruction.* Upper Saddle River, NJ: Prentice Hall.

Beaver, Joetta. 2001. *Developmental Reading Assessment, K–3.* Parsippany, NJ: Celebration.

Black, Paul, and Dylan Wiliam. 1998. "Inside the Black Box: Raising Standards Through Classroom Assessment." *Phi Delta Kappan* 80 (2): 139–148.

Calkins, Lucy McCormick. 2001. *The Art of Teaching Reading.* New York: Longman.

———. 2003a. *Units of Study for Primary Writing: A Yearlong Curriculum.* Portsmouth, NH: Heinemann.

———. 2003b. "The Nuts and Bolts of Teaching Writing." In *Units of Study for Primary Writing.* Portsmouth NH: Heinemann.

Clay, Marie M. 1993. *An Observation Survey of Early Literacy Achievement.* Portsmouth, NH: Heinemann.

D'Agostino, Jerome V., and Judith A. Murphy. 2004. "A Meta-analysis of Reading Recovery in United States Schools." *Educational Evaluation and Policy Analysis* 26 (1): 23–38.

Darling-Hammond, Linda. 1990. "Instructional Policy into Practice: 'The Power of the Bottom over the Top.'" *Educational Evaluation and Policy Analysis* 12 (3): 233–241.

———. 2000. "Teacher Quality and Student Achievement: A Review of State Policy Evidence." *Education Policy Analysis Archives* 8 (1).

Deno, S. L., and D. Marston. 2006. "Curriculum-Based Measurement of Oral Reading: An Indicator of Growth in Fluency." In *What Research Has to Say About Fluency Instruction*, ed. S. J. Samuels and A. E. Farstrup (pp. 179–203). Newark, DE: International Reading Association.

Dorn, Linda J., Cathy French, and Tammy Jones. 1998. *Apprenticeship in Literacy: Transitions Across Reading and Writing.* Portland, ME: Stenhouse.

DuFour, Richard, Rebecca DuFour, Robert Eaker, and Gayle Karhanek. 2004. *Whatever It Takes: How Professional Learning Communities Respond When Kids Don't Learn.* Bloomington, IN: National Educational Service.

DuFour, Richard, Rebecca DuFour, Robert Eaker, and Thomas Many. 2006. *Learning by Doing: A Handbook for Professional Learning Communities at Work.* Bloomington, IN: Solution Tree.

Easton, Lois B. 2004. *Powerful Designs for Professional Learning.* Oxford, OH: National Staff Development Council.

Erikson, H. Lynn 2002. *Concept-Based Curriculum and Instruction: Teaching Beyond Facts*. Thousand Oaks, CA: Corwin.

Fink, Rosalie P. 2006. *Why Jane and Johnny Couldn't Read—And How They Learned*. Newark, DE: International Reading Association.

Fountas, Irene C. and Gay Su Pinnell. 1996. *Guided Reading: Good First Teaching for All Children*. Portsmouth, NH: Heinemann.

———. 2001. *Guiding Readers and Writers, Grades 3–6: Teaching Comprehension, Genre, and Content Literacy*. Portsmouth, NH: Heinemann.

———. 2006. *Leveled Books, K–8: Matching Books to Readers for Effective Teaching*. Portsmouth, NH: Heinemann.

Frankfurter, Felix. 1950. Dissenting opinion in *Dennis v. United States*.

Fry, Edward B. 1980. "The New Instant Word List." *The Reading Teacher* 34: 284–290.

Fry, E., J. Kress, and D. Fountoukidis. 2004. *The Reading Teacher's Book of Lists*. Englewood Cliffs, NJ: Prentice Hall.

Fuchs, Lynn S., Stanley L. Deno, and Phyllis K. Mirkin. 1984. "Effects of Frequent Curriculum-Based Measurement on Pedagogy, Student Achievement, and Student Awareness of Learning." *American Educational Research Journal* 21: 449–460.

Fullan, Michael D. 1982. *The Meaning of Educational Change*. New York: Teachers College Press.

———. 1997. *What's Worth Fighting For?* New York: Teachers College Press.

———. 2003. *The Moral Imperative of School Leadership*. Thousand Oaks, CA: Corwin.

Ganske, Kathy. 2000. *Word Journeys: Assessment-Guided Phonics, Spelling, and Vocabulary Instruction*. New York: Guilford.

Gladwell, Malcolm. 2000. *The Tipping Point: How Little Things Can Make a Big Difference*. Boston: Little Brown.

Graves, Donald. 1994. *A Fresh Look at Writing*. Portsmouth, NH: Heinemann.

Guthrie, John T., Allen Wigfield, Pedro Barbosa, Kathleen C. Perencevich, Ana Taboada, Marcia H. Davis, Nicole T. Scafidda, and Stephen Tonks. 2004. "Increasing Reading Comprehension and Engagement Through Concept Oriented Reading Instruction." *Journal of Educational Psychology* 96 (3): 403–423.

Harvey, Stephanie. 2004. *Strategic Thinking: Reading and Responding, Grades 4–8*. Video recording. Portland, ME: Stenhouse.

Keene, Ellin. 2006. "Literacy Learning: What Is Essential?" Presentation at Lakota Literacy VIEW conference, West Chester, Ohio.

Lambert, Linda. 2003. *Leadership Capacity for Lasting School Improvement*. Alexandria, VA: Association for Supervision and Curriculum Development.

Leslie, Lauren, and JoAnne Caldwell. 2000. *Qualitative Reading Inventory–4*. 4th ed. Boston: Allyn and Bacon.

Marzano, Robert J. 2007. *The Art and Science of Teaching: A Complete Framework for Effective Instruction*. Alexandria, VA: Association for Supervision and Curriculum Development.

Marzano, Robert J., and John S. Kendall. 1998. *Awash in a Sea of Standards*. Aurora, CO: Mid-continent Research for Education and Learning.

McNulty, Raymond. 2007. "Essential Learnings for School Reinvention." Presentation at the Model Schools Conference. Washington, DC.

Miller, Debbie. 2002. *Happy Reading! Creating a Predictable Structure for Joyful Teaching and Learning*. Video recording. Portland, ME: Stenhouse.

National Staff Development Council. 2005. "If Not a Workshop, Then What?" *Tools for Schools*. Dec./Jan.: 8.

Ohio Department of Education. 2007. "Alignment Toolbox for the English Language Arts." http://www.ode.state. oh.us/GD/Templates/Pages/ODE/ODEDetail.aspx?Page=3&TopicRelationID=720&ContentID=1918&Content=36594.

Pearson, P. David, Janice A. Dole, Gerald Duffy, and Laura R. Roehler. 1992. "Developing Expertise in Reading Comprehension: What Should Be Taught and How Should It Be Taught?" In *What Research Has to Say to the Teacher of Reading*, ed. Alan E. Farstrup and S. Jay Samuels. 2nd ed. Newark, DE: International Reading Association.

Pearson, P. David, and Linda Fielding. 1991. "Comprehension Instruction." In *Handbook of Reading Research*, ed. Rebecca Barr, Michael L. Kamil, Peter Mosenthal, and P. David Pearson (Vol. 2, pp. 819–860). New York: Longman.

Pearson, P. David, and Margaret C. Gallagher. 1983. "Instruction of Reading Comprehension." *Contemporary Educational Psychology* 8:317–344.

Pearson, P. David, and Dale D. Johnson. 1978. *Teaching Reading Comprehension*. New York: Holt, Rinehart and Winston.

Pressley, Michael, Carla J. Johnson, Sonya Symons, Jacqueline A. McGoldrick, and Janice A. Kurita. 1989. "Strategies That Improve Children's Memory and Comprehension of Text." *Elementary School Journal* 90 (1): 3–32.

Pressley, Michael, Richard Allington, Ruth Wharton-MacDonald, Cathy C. Block, and Lesley M. Morrow. 2001. *Learning to Read: Lessons from Exemplary First-Grade Classrooms*. New York: Guilford.

Rasinski, Timothy B. 2003. *The Fluent Reader: Oral Reading Strategies for Building Word Recognition, Fluency, and Comprehension*. New York: Scholastic.

Reeves, Douglas B. 2002. *The Leader's Guide to Standards: A Blueprint for Educational Equity and Excellence*. San Francisco: Jossey-Bass.

Schmoker, Mike. 1996. *Results: The Key to Continuous School Improvement*. Alexandria, VA: Association for Supervision and Curriculum Development.

Sparks, Dennis. 2002. "In Search of Heroes: Give Educators a Place on the Pedestal." Interview with Roland Barth. *Journal of Staff Development* 23 (1): 46–50.

———. 2005. "The Final 2%: What It Takes to Create Profound Change in Leaders." *Journal of Staff Development* 26 (2): 8–15.

Stiggins, Richard, J. Arter, J. Chappuis, and S. Chappuis. 2004. *Classroom Assessment for Student Learning: Doing It Right— Using It Well*. Portland, OR: Assessment Training Institute.

Swanson, H. Lee, and Maureen Hoskyn. 1998. "Experimental Intervention Research on Students with Learning Disabilities: A Meta-analysis of Outcomes." *Review of Educational Research* 68 (3): 277–321.

Taylor, Barbara M., P. David Pearson, Debra S. Peterson, and Michael C. Rodriguez. 2003. "Reading Growth in High-Poverty Classrooms: The Influence of Teacher Practices That Encourage Cognitive Engagement in Literacy Learning." *Elementary School Journal* 104:3–28.

Tichy, Noel. 1997. *The Leadership Engine: How Winning Companies Build Leaders at Every Level*. New York: Harper Business.

U.S. Department of Education Institute of Education Sciences. 2005. *Identifying and Implementing Educational Practices Supported by Rigorous Evidence: A User Friendly Guide*. Washington, DC.

Vaughn, Sharon, Sylvia Linan-Thompson, Kamiar Kouzekanani, Diane P. Bryant, Shirley Dickson, and Shelley A. Blozis. 2003. "Reading Instruction Grouping for Students with Reading Difficulties." *Remedial and Special Education* 24 (5): 301–315.

Waterman, Robert. 1987. *The Renewal Factor: How the Best Get and Keep the Competitive Edge*. New York: Bantam.

Zimmermann, Susan, and Chryse Hutchins. 2003. *Seven Keys to Comprehension: How to Help Your Kids Read It and Get It!* New York: Three Rivers.

Index